The less stress book

How to turn stress to your advantage.

The less stress book

How to turn stress to your advantage.

A CONSUMERS' INSTITUTE GUIDE

The Less Stress Book is published by
Consumers' Institute of New Zealand Inc
Private Bag 6996, 39 Webb Street, Wellington 6035
tel: 04 384 7963
fax: 04 385 8752
email: chiefexec@consumer.org.nz

Copyright David Winsborough and Kay Allen 1997

No material in this publication may
be reproduced in any form without
the written permission of the publisher.

Printed by: GP Print Limited
Design and typesetting: Mission Hall Design Group
Editor: Jane Parkin

ISBN 0- 908658-36-2

Contents

	Introduction	1
1	What is this thing called stress?	6
2	The physical stress reaction	14
3	The health consequences of stress	32
4	Stress and the brain	41
5	Stress and your approach to life	53
6	Changing your thinking	68
7	Physical relaxation	88
8	Dealing with strong feelings	104
9	The CALM approach	113
10	Where to from here?	130
	Afterword	132

THE LESS STRESS BOOK

Dedication and Acknowledgements

This book is dedicated to all the clients who courageously made changes to their lives and from whom we have learnt so much.

We wish to thank the following people: Jane Parkin for teaching us how to write in English; Keith Petrie for not writing it with us; and to Amanda Smith, Richard Bishop, Elizabeth and Finn for waiting so long to talk to us again. We would also like to mention our colleagues in our practice: Hi y'all.

THE LESS STRESS BOOK

Introduction

Is stress really a problem in modern life? Here is a sample of views from a diverse range of sources. At the time of writing this book we had just completed a series of stress management seminars for a large New Zealand corporation. To the surprise of the training department which offered them, the enrolments numbered more than 90% of all staff.

In 1994 a study conducted at the University of Auckland Medical School found that heart attack victims overwhelmingly attributed the cause of their coronary illness to stress. Not high blood pressure, not cholesterol or poor diet, but stress.

An Australian study examining healthy lifestyle choices amongst immigrant women attributed much of the obesity evident in the group to the stress inherent in living in a new country with limited community support networks.

Various studies of attendance at GPs' surgeries around the world indicates that anywhere between 30% and 60% of patient visits are accounted for by so-called vague symptoms – sleeplessness, various aches and pains, tension, relationship issues and so on. Most of these symptoms have no clear disease link, and are attributed by the authors to the catch-all 'stress reactions'.

A 1995 report from the Family Violence Commission valued the cost of violence-related problems in New Zealand at around $1.2 billion and perhaps up to $5 billion every year. Violence is an issue that is affected by many factors, but the report's main author, economist Suzanne Snively, said that 'the stresses and strains of modern life' clearly impact on the way in which men cope (or not).

Clearly, lots of organisations and individuals believe stress to be a problem, and much has already been written on the subject. Why, then, another book about it?

Many of the publications we have seen are of poor quality – the advice they give is about as meaningful as that picked up from advice pages in magazines. Proposing simplistic solutions to problems that have multiple causes is at best unhelpful. In many books stress is also needlessly sensationalised, and fear messages – 'Stress Kills!' – used as a selling tool. Most books don't offer an up-to-date view of stress that is based on sound scientific principles and theory. If they did, it would become clear that there is no need to get stressed about stress.

This book is different. We have blended modern scientific findings with our experience as practising psychologists to show that stress is inevitable, normal and not to be feared. Stress is nothing more than a bodily reaction and part of what it means to be alive. It is certainly possible to reduce the reactions we have to stressful things, but we believe that attempting to cut all stress from our lives simply has no meaning.

Instead we encourage readers to develop a much longer-term view of their stress management, especially in relation to those stressful events about which we can do nothing. Ours is therefore a two-pronged approach. In this book we look at: 1) attitudinal and lifestyle approaches which aim to reduce stress and promote joy in living; and 2) exercises and approaches that offer practical solutions to reducing our reactions to stress and lowering its negative impact on our lives.

Real change involves understanding how and why we got stressed in the first place and instituting life changes to ensure that we don't end up suffering again six months later. So considerable coverage is given to exploring how things like our expectations of life, our everyday thoughts and even 'patterns' of behaviour need to change to reduce stress.

We vastly prefer the idea that individuals manage their health with the aim of enjoying life to the fullest in their particular circumstances. Healthy eating, adequate exercise, relaxation and sensible thinking, and developing a sense of meaning and purpose in life can head off problems before they occur or become serious. We cannot avoid stress, and life does not play fair. Making the best of whatever we have to face embodies the concept of wellness.

How to use this book
We have tried to make using this book as easy as possible.

You don't have to read it from cover to cover. You may browse and choose exercises or suggestions that are of special interest to you. These are clearly marked by either a ✋ or a ✏️. (More about these symbols below.)

Reading the whole book right through will, however, lead to a much deeper understanding of the way stress works in the body and how it affects our health, thinking and behaviour. *We strongly encourage you to read the whole book.* In our professional work we have learned that the people who do best are those who continue learning and changing even though they've stopped the immediate bad feeling or situation that led to their seeking help. Stress is rarely the result of only one event: take the time to examine your situation thoroughly and seek to learn from it.

This highlights the focus of the book, which is unashamedly about changing psychological stress. We mention the value of eating well, moderating alcohol intake and getting plenty of exercise, but do not dwell on them. This is not to underestimate how important these factors are; in fact they are at least as important as learning the techniques described in this book.

You may care to read Jenny Pierce's book *Eat your Stress Away*, Reed Books, 1996, Leslie Kenton's *10 Day De-Stress Plan*, Ebury Press, 1994, or Hilary Tupling's *A Weight Off Your Mind*, Sydney, Baitam, 1991. All of these books have excellent advice and information concerning the relationship between eating patterns and stress.

We have used symbols through the book to make reading it a little easier. The symbols mean:

 a handy idea or practical tip for you to use and try

 a key point or a real-life example

 a chunk of theory or psychological background – interesting but not essential

 an exercise for you to complete

 a book we found useful or that contains a fuller description than in this text

THE PHILOSOPHY OF OUR APPROACH

Just before Christmas 1994 all court judges in New Zealand were awarded a pay increase of up to 6% that was partly based upon what the Higher Salaries Commission called the 'stress they face with busy schedules and demanding workloads'.

The practice of awarding money for stress problems seems to us misguided. The logic behind it seems to be one of admitting that the job leads to poorer-quality family life, health consequences or burnout, but that changing or adapting the job to fit better with human lifestyles is less preferable than buying silence or tolerance from the damaged individuals. This same tactic has also occurred in other professions, notably teaching; in New Zealand several 'one-off' payments of between $1000 and $3000 were made to compensate teachers for stress.

We do not doubt that judges and teachers have very stressful jobs, but claiming that a pay increase can compensate or alleviate the situation is idiotic. Far better that the extra money is spent on either the extra resources required or equipping people to manage stress better.

So this book has a strong message that the power to make real change rests with the individual affected. Too often it seems that people abdicate to others the ability to change, and then complain because the company or boss or government won't accept their view that the system is unfair. By all means complain if the 'system is unfair', but take responsibility for yourself now. Don't wait for systems, bosses, husbands, wives, parents or governments to change before you act.

CHAPTER 1

What is this thing called Stress?

HOW DO PEOPLE SEE STRESS?

There seems to be a lot of hype about stress. Reading a range of books about it will demonstrate a curious thing: they will tell you either that you should be worried about imminent stress-related disease or, conversely, that your stress should be an energising experience, a positive thing. The field, apparently, is wide open.

We decided to find out how people actually characterised their beliefs about stress.

We asked more than 200 people who attended our stress workshops how they thought and felt about stress. In small groups of between three and five people we asked them to list all the words that came immediately to mind when they thought of the word 'stress'. Then we asked them to assign their words to either a positive or negative category.

The ratio of positive to negative words was around 1:20, which means that for every one positive word, there were 20 negative ones. Even allowing for the fact that these people were attending a seminar to cope with stress, we were amazed by the firmness of their view that stress is overwhelmingly negative. In the table below we have reproduced a typical example of what emerged.

HOW DO PEOPLE VIEW STRESS?

Positive	Negative
normal, exciting, adrenaline rush	hassle, problems, tired, angry, illness, pressures, bosses, ageing, worry, tight, strung-out, headache, overworked, money, arguments, strained, poor management, long hours, never-ending, anxious, yelling, pissed-off

Well frankly, we agree. Those words do describe what it feels like to be stressed. For most people the experience is decidedly unpleasant.

The reason is a delightful mix of reality and psychological trick. Stress is *real* because unyielding pressure leads to physical changes in the body and mental exhaustion that combine to leave us feeling really bad. But it is a *trick* because our beliefs (often founded on myth and misinformation) about stress cause us to *expect* to feel bad, and this in turn makes us especially alert to negative signs or feelings of distress.

Let's clear away some of the confusion about stress. We have listed below some of the myths and misconceptions that we have heard through the years from our clients. Alongside these we have offered some counter-arguments. If you are currently inclined to believe some of the statements in the column on the left, we hope you'll have changed your mind by the end of this book.

Test your beliefs against some research findings.

Myth	Truth
Stress happens only to weak people.	Stress happens to all of us. It is a basic life response to the need to cope or adapt.
Stress is just a mental thing.	Stress is a complex mix of physical changes that interact with how we think and process information.
Stress is a bad thing.	Why? Stress channels energy to help us cope or adapt – is that bad?
Stress is exaggerated – nothing really happens.	Stress may be exaggerated by self-serving media, but it is very real.
Once this hassle goes away I'll be fine.	Stress is cumulative in its effects. It also takes some time for the body's reaction to subside.
Stress happens to you, and there's nothing you can do to prevent it.	No, stress is a blend of what happens in our lives and how we adapt or respond to those events. You certainly can prevent yourself becoming so stressed.
You can't get stressed if you are doing something you like.	Yes you can. The same response underlies how we react to most challenging events in our lives.

DEFINING STRESS

We want to clarify what we mean by 'stress' because we use the word to refer to a specific set of circumstances and processes that are mainly physical. Most people know from experience what feeling stressed is like. In fact evidence from around the world shows that the gross signs and symptoms of distress don't vary much from race to race or country to country. We find, however, that people use 'stress' in a sloppy fashion – to describe feelings or to describe a cause, or even something someone else does to you, as in 'You're stressing me out.'

Test this with a simple experiment. Ask the next 10 people you come into contact with what they understand by the term 'stress'.

When we do this experiment with people attending our courses, we find that defining stress seems to be surprisingly hard. People can say whether they are or aren't stressed, but can't tell us quite what it is. Our results are typically like this:

About half of the people asked tell us of their current *problems:* the kids; the mortgage; the fight they had with their parents, their wife, husband, boss; the workload they're under; the pressures; and on, and on, and on…

Around a third will tell us of the *symptoms* they are suffering: how tired they have been feeling, how they don't seem to be coping so well with their work, the irritability of their spouse, their sleep being poor, the headaches, pains, colds, and on, and on, and on…

Sharp readers will have spotted that some of the symptoms look a lot like problems. They are. Stress is cumulative and the results of stress can also become the causes of more stress.

Of the remainder, one or two always say something like: 'Stress? I never suffer from it. That's a problem suffered by weaklings. I've always said, 'if you can't stand the heat, get out of the kitchen.'

So stress is used to describe the causes, symptoms and the workings of our minds. That's quite a range. Unfortunately it is exactly the same with scientists. Their views of stress vary even more widely – and, being scientists, none can quite agree on what it is they are referring to.

SO, WHAT IS STRESS, REALLY?

Stress is not something that happens *to* us. It isn't being fired, arguing with our families, having the in-laws for the whole of Christmas or even waking up and discovering that it's Monday morning. All of these things are called *stressors* (or changes, or hassles, or problems, or pressures).

Stress is the whole *generalised* response of our minds and bodies to stressors, or those events in our lives that mean we have to change or cope in some way.

By generalised response we mean that although the stress involved in winning Lotto or the stress of being late are experienced differently by each individual, the same basic biochemical and physiological changes underlie the specific response.

At least as far as our bodies are concerned, stress is a *dumb* response – we turn on the same bodily reaction, more or less, no matter what the stimulus is. This response varies only in degree. So the person who is late for an important meeting and breaks into a sweat and feels their heart pounding has the same basic response as the person who has just won Lotto.

We can now properly define stress as:

Our generalised reaction to any event, person, place or thought, memory or belief which requires us to cope or adapt.

See the seminal work by the 'father' of stress research, Hans Selye, *The Stress of Life*, NY, McGraw-Hill, 1956. If you are deeply interested in the relationship between stress and meaning, then take the trouble to read an inspiring book by Viktor Frankl, *Man's Search for Meaning*, Boston, Beacon Press, 1992.

Although the basic bodily reaction is pretty much the same for everyone, stress is not the same *experience* for all of us. Knowing that this physical reaction occurs in response to a variety of different events provides an important clue as to how our minds enter the stress equation: we can even say that the degree of stress we end up with depends a great deal on the *meaning* that we attach to our experiences.

That explains why the very same stressor may cause different people to react in completely different ways.

This was illustrated when we once conducted counselling interviews with a number of people who had just been told that the office in which they worked was to be closed and that they would all be losing their jobs, although there would be severance money. Some workers burst into tears. Some just stared blankly with their mouths open, while others smiled delightedly. When we spoke to those who had smiled we discovered that for a variety of reasons they saw this as a great chance to change the direction of their lives – early retirement for one, the opportunity to move to another city for another. This underscores one of the most important points about stress:

How we think about events and react to them determines how stressful they are.

Young police college graduates provide a great example of this point. At the start of their careers they often find their work exhilarating and challenging. After many years of putting their lives in danger, however, and with the added responsibilities of family life, many find that the same car chases that were once exciting can seem unnecessary and terrifying.

Stress that is too great or that goes on for too long can wear our resistance down, leading to *changed* reactions and feelings.

Stress is not a single event, but must be understood in relation to all the events and processes of our lives.

Remember, *stressors* are the things that lead to our reactions; the *stress response* is the physical and mental changes that occur in response to stressors; and *symptoms* are the outcomes that we experience. The most important realisation is that *stress is the whole process we have described.*

Viewing stress as a *process* is important, because it tells us that all of these events exist in relation to each other. Changing any one of them will always affect the others in the process. Stress is everywhere!

Where is stress?

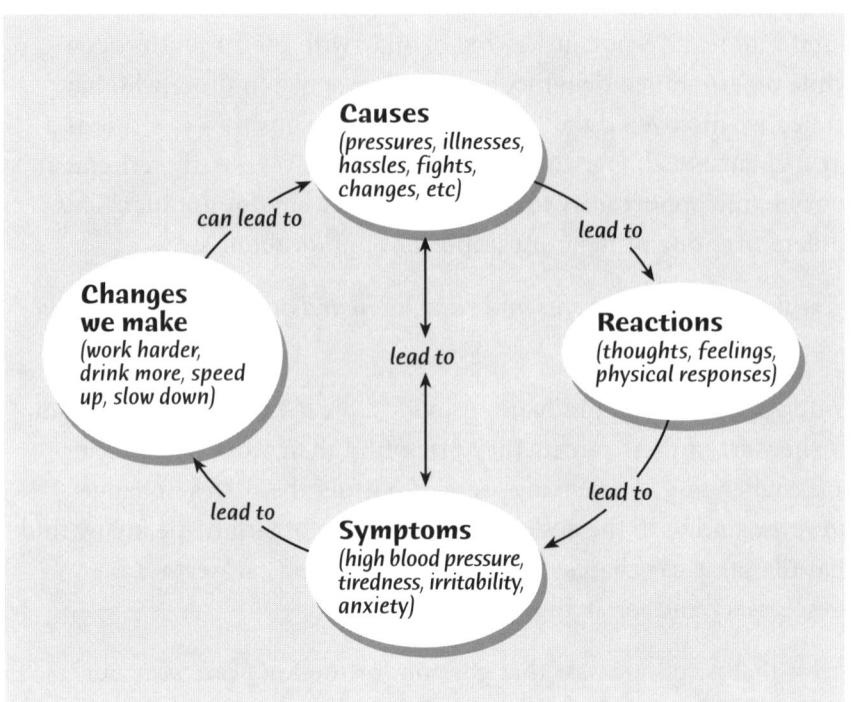

Take the example of a woman who is worried about the amount of work she has to get through. This *cause* leads to difficulty sleeping, which is a quite natural *reaction* – she lies in bed turning things over and worrying a lot. Not sleeping leads to her feeling tired and a bit anxious about not having enough sleep, both of which are common *symptoms* for people who are sleep-deprived. Being tired and anxious, however, causes her to work less effectively, so she *changes* her normal pattern, stays later at work to catch up, which leads to her feeling resentful about her company and worrying that she can't do all the tasks required…

Symptoms of stress, such as tiredness and irritability, can actually become stressors in themselves.

Similarly, even coping strategies that may make us feel better in the short term, perhaps like drinking alcohol to relax, or avoiding an unpleasant encounter, can also cause stressful situations later on.

THE ART OF STRESS

Stress is a term researchers borrowed from engineering, where it refers to the forces that cause something to change or deform. Strain is the result of too much stress, or stress in the wrong place.

Ironically, taking away stress, which is what most people want to do, can have the opposite effect. To mend a faltering stone arch, architects may *add* more load to it to bind the bricks more tightly.

So too with human beings. We are not designed to be in a tensionless state, free from all pressures and loads. The right amount of challenge and tension helps provide the conditions for an active, moving and fulfilled life. You cannot live 'stress free', so don't fool yourself into assuming that no stress will lead to a calm and happy life.

The art lies in attaining a balance between the various forces and events in your life – physical, emotional, social and spiritual. Working through the exercises in this book will help you determine just what is 'right' for you.

CHAPTER 2

The physical stress reaction

A supermarket is not the sort of place in which we'd expect to see the physical nature of the stress response demonstrated, yet one of us recently observed in an Australian supermarket a wonderful example of stress in action. On a hot, hot Queensland afternoon a very young mother was slowly pushing a shopping trolley, herding two children at her feet, while her third child, a baby, yelled urgently in the carry tray. Her oldest child was rushing ahead, pulling items off the shelf and generally causing extreme stress to the shop assistants who had to smother the urge to smother the child. The child seemed oblivious to the mayhem she was causing, raced further ahead and then disappeared around the corner of the aisle. The mother looked dispirited, tired and frazzled. As she came around the top of the aisle, though, she caught sight of the oldest one scampering out the supermarket doors into the busy carpark. Instantly the formerly tired mother was transformed into an athlete: she flashed across the supermarket, vaulted the checkout railing, sprinted out the doors into the carpark and, weaving between cars, swept the youngster up. She ran back to the supermarket, put the child in the trolley and burst into tears!

(It is quite common for emotional reactions to come *after* the stressful situation has passed, when we are psychologically safe again. It seems that during stress we may suppress strong emotions or feelings while we deal with the situation, only to let go of the control after the danger has passed or the situation has been dealt with. This can result in physical reactions, such as shaking, weakness or headaches, but may also appear in emotional reactions, such as weeping or, sometimes, inappropriate laughter.)

The amazing transformation demonstrated by the young mother is what the stress response is all about – survival. Within seconds of perceiving a threat (the child loose in a carpark and liable to be flattened), our hero was 'activated' from a low-level state (tired and frazzled) to a high-energy state. Her heart rate and blood pressure soared. Her breathing changed to a fast, shallow pattern designed to charge her blood with oxygen. The circulation of blood itself would have changed, flowing into the muscles of her legs, preparing her for running. If we could have seen her eyes, we would have noticed they were wide and her pupils were dilated, allowing more light (and information) in. Her thinking also changed, so that she concentrated on what was necessary. At that time she wouldn't have been thinking of how tired she was, or what was on the television or how many bills she had to pay. Other things would have changed in her body as it went to 'action stations'. Muscle tone (tension) increased, hormones such as corticosteroids (for muscle repair) and endorphins (for pain control) flowed into her system.

This 'tired mother' had become galvanised for action, focused solely on resolving the threat to her child.

Triggered by adrenaline, her body would have remained in this activated state for hours, although she may have remained unaware of it as her heart rate and breathing pattern gradually returned to normal. Other people may have noticed the young mother remained unsettled, jumpy and irritable. This effect would have lasted until the chemicals and hormones unleashed had worked their way through her system.

STRESS IS PHYSICAL

It is obvious from the description above that stress is very much a *physical event*, even though we may also experience emotional upset as a result of stressful situations.

In the 1930s it was recognised that the human body, when placed under a variety of stressful situations, displayed a standard pattern of response. No matter what the challenge, the same basic organ changes, blood flow, hormone release and so on occurred. This was a very surprising discovery – the more so because it appeared to be similar in nearly every other animal studied.

Hans Selye, *The Stress of Life*, NY, McGraw-Hill, was the person who studied this finding most. He studied stress in rats by pulling their tails. Subsequently he generalised his findings to humans (but he didn't pull their tails.)

But the human stress response is different in that while it is triggered by external events, such as a physical threat (fire breaks out – what will we do?) or a physical challenge (climbing stairs), it also responds to internal factors, such as threats to our self-esteem (a colleague says you haven't the brains to be in your position) or anticipation of feared events (you've been asked to deliver a talk to 100 people). The fact that we get stressed by non-physical threats is perhaps the factor that most differentiates us from other animals.

THE PHYSICAL RESPONSE DESCRIBED

The stress response is a major part of our defence system. Its first task is to improve response times for various body parts, and to change the manner in which we think. Kept in reserve, it is a useful part of being human, a quick-fire body preparation device. Activated too often, however, it can become toxic and damaging, affecting our health and emotional well-being.

You don't need to know about exactly what happens in your body – but it may be useful, and certainly will be interesting. If you want to, skip ahead to the symptoms of stress at the end of this chapter.

As the body responds to these events, a marvellous and bewildering array of changes occurs in the body. The stress response links nearly all the major organs, endocrine (hormone), brain and muscular systems, and encourages them to perform in a strictly patterned way. This is a built-in system response, or instinct, bequeathed to us by our ancestors from millions of years in the past. We cannot turn it off or remove it – we can only learn how to use it and modify it.

Try this simple exercise to help focus on what happens inside your body when in a threatening situation:

Think back to a time when you had a real fright, or to when you were under some intense performance demand. For example, it may have been a confrontation in the course of your work, a car accident or near miss, or a scary thrill in a high-risk sport such as parachuting, skiing or climbing. Or perhaps you had to do a threatening thing, like speaking to a large audience.

Allow yourself to re-live the event, to recall the sights and sounds and feelings you experienced.

Write down all the *physical sensations* you can remember.

These exercises and others will help you identify your own pattern of response.

Write down any *thoughts or feelings* you recall.

Write down how your *behaviour* changed.

Now write down how you felt as you *remembered* the event today.

Now think back to a time when you had a real thrill (such as at a scary movie), or to when you were tense but excited (asking someone out for the first time, or at the start of an important game or race).

Write down all the *physical sensations* you can remember.

Write down any *thoughts or feelings* you recall.

Write down how your *behaviour* changed.

_____

_____

_____

Now write down how you felt as you *remembered* the event today.

_____

_____

_____

What did you notice? Were there similarities in terms of what your body experienced? Were your thoughts different? Did even the *memory* of what occurred produce the faintest stirrings of the same feelings?

Most people notice similar things occurred in their bodies during a stressful event. Perhaps you noticed that your heart sped up, or that you were breathing faster, or that you tended to sweat. Check below and compare what you wrote with the list of 'typical' responses:

Physical sensations in stress reactions

What we may notice	Why this happens in our body
Our heart races or pounds. Our chest feels tight and we may feel flushed.	Our heart rate increases and our blood pressure rises to carry oxygen and fuel to the muscles, clearing unwanted waste much faster than normal.
We pant or our breathing is panicky.	Breathing becomes more shallow and rapid, which enables us to get oxygen into our blood quickly.
Our muscles feel tense and tight and may ache or feel painful. We may have a sore stomach. We feel twitchy or feel we want to move.	The muscles tense, especially the thighs, back, stomach, shoulders, arms and jaw, and blood is directed to the major large-muscle groups. This prepares the body for explosive action.
Our sight becomes acute and we focus on only one thing - we develop tunnel vision.	The pupils dilate to let in more light, and the other senses are heightened. This is to enable us to scan as much information as possible.

We have butterflies in our stomach, there are various gurgles, bubbles and rumbles. We may have wind and nausea.	The stomach and gut slow digestion because all energy is directed towards fight or flight.
We may have a feeling of lightness, a sense of urgency or speed, a 'high' excited sensation. We feel we cannot keep still, that we want some 'action'.	The body releases adrenaline, other hormones and steroids into the bloodstream. These speed up our response times and trigger the reactions described. The body's own painkillers and steroids ensure we can continue to move, even if injured, and promote fast healing.
We feel we have energy to spare. Our hands and feet are cold.	The liver releases stored fats and sugars for energy. The blood flow to our hands and feet is reduced to prevent excessive bleeding if they are injured.
Our concentration improves. Time seems to slow down.	The blood is directed to the brain for faster thinking. Our quick reactions make it seem as if time has slowed.
We get hot or cold sweats, especially on the hands, feet, face, armpits or groin.	Perspiration increases to cool the body.
We experience the need to pass urine or a bowel motion.	The stomach contents and intestines go into spasm to get rid of 'unnecessary baggage'.
We feel fear or excitement. Other feelings wash over us.	The brain interprets our reactions. We become more emotionally reactive.

The stress reaction outlined above is tightly tied to what is called the *fight or flight* response. This is a term coined by the researcher Hans Selye, and summarises what he thought all this physical activity was for: preparing the organism to deal with a threat through fighting for its life, or preserving its life through running away.

It is theorised that before human brains had evolved to the point that we could invent ways to control our environment, nature provided us with a 'quick and dirty' response system for quickly arousing and preparing our bodies to fight or to flee from the occasional life-threatening situation. Nature also provided most other creatures with a comparable system, perhaps to give everything a fighting chance. Certainly we can observe a similar response when animals are threatened or cornered. If you have a pet you may like to observe what happens when it is suddenly scared. Changes in physical appearance, fast movements, quicker reactions and changes in temperament are reliable signs of stress.

So, the fight or flight response operates through some of the more 'primitive' parts of our brain that developed early on in the evolutionary process. This part of the brain directly influences the performance of many basic bodily functions, such as heartbeat, breathing, the flow of hormones and so on. Think of it as the regulatory part of the brain that keeps things ticking over *without our consciously thinking of them.*

Time Distortion

At times of extreme stress, people report visual distortions, as if things seem larger, or that time seems to slow down and events move in slow motion.

In one of our cases, a police officer confronted a young man who was drunk and high on solvents (in this case CRC and glue). The youth had a gun and the policeman reported watching as it was aimed towards him. He described the gun as: 'Huge, like it was a giant toy, with a barrel that was a foot across. As I moved towards him I remember seeing everything really clearly, and it was in slow motion. I saw him lift the gun and I could see him start to pull the trigger...'

The officer, needless to say, survived.

The explanation for the 'slowing of time' that he experienced is found in the brain. Under stress the eye dilates to let in more light, allowing us to see more clearly and notice far more detail. The way information is processed in the brain also changes and 'short-circuits' its normal route. At the same time the brain stops a lot of the mental chatter and worry that often constitutes our thoughts, and instead focuses solely on dealing with the information that is most crucial to us at the time. This means we process information more quickly, but have the illusion of time unfolding slowly.

It is important to remember that this is an automatic reaction or a type of reflexive, instinctive response. Many people hope for a life free from stress, but that is an anatomical impossibility. The best we can hope for is to understand the response and learn to live *with it*, instead of struggling to ignore it or subdue it.

When the stress response was investigated more deeply, a curious anomaly emerged. It seems that the improvement in performance holds true *only up to a certain level of stress and for a limited time*. If the stress gets too great, or there are too many demands on us, our performance deteriorates. This observation is immortalised in the names of the people who first reported it: the Yerkes-Dodson Law.

The Yerkes-Dodson Law

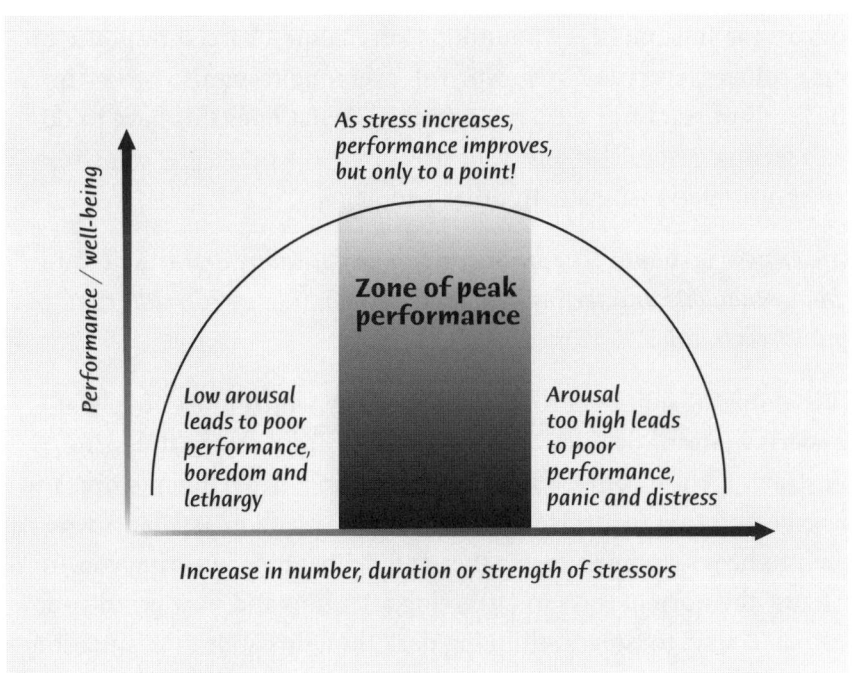

Modern athletes use this law to change their psychological and physical arousal at the right level for top performance. They do this through calming routines and breathing exercises to reduce arousal; coaches may 'hype' or 'psych' their charges through pre-game talks or by yelling and cajoling from the sidelines.

It is also easy to see this law in operation in everyday family life. A parent might cope really well looking after one child during the day. If the child has two or three friends to stay, then the parent speeds up, monitoring all the kids' activities and generally turning on a real show. But if we add more stress by turning the TV up loud, or having more kids arrive, or the telephone going, then look out. 'Performance' drops away as the now frazzled and stressed parent starts to yell and *control* the children, trying to reduce the pressure to a manageable level again.

WHERE IS THE HARM THEN?

Stress is a *normal* response. We have seen that there are times when it is very adaptive and useful. At other times it seems quite unnecessary to have the full-on, heart-pounding, adrenaline-charged response in our ordinary, everyday lives. Nor will everyone recognise 'stress' in the kinds of reactions we have described. What does this have to do with feeling irritable or angry, or pressured at work? How can stress affect our relationships with other people?

The answer is simple. The stress reaction is not smart and it is activated via our thoughts and feelings, and will respond to any stimulus that 'pushes its buttons'.

This annoying quirk is probably the path by which most people in modern western societies cause themselves unnecessary stress. To illustrate, picture yourself as the customer in a department store. You have been trying to attract the attention of two shop assistants who seem to be gossiping to each other and deliberately ignoring you. You exhaust the normal ways of attracting attention and now grind your teeth and start to 'steam', thinking dark thoughts about the situation and those arrogant shop assistants. *Because of those angry thoughts you are having to work in order to suppress your 'primitive' emotions and the urge to teach those shop assistants a lesson they won't forget.*

Michael Douglas gave a revealing portrayal of how a man who had been stressed too much could react in the movie *Falling Down*.

What you would like to do is yell, stamp your feet or throw something at them (this is our 'fight' reaction). It isn't acceptable to inflict primitive violence on shop assistants, so you 'restrain yourself', but your body knows nothing of these social niceties. The stress response will be turned on. You may not consciously be aware of it, but it will be experienced in rising body temperature, tightening muscles or feelings of rage.

Almost anything that is demanding (physically or psychologically) will activate the stress response. To be sure it won't be the full response every time, but in various degrees and ways the body's response system will be activated. The 'sickening' irony is that although we activate the response time and time again, *we seldom carry through the demand for real action.* If we did we might use up the potentially damaging by-products of stress.

The damage from stress occurs because stress is turned on too easily and we suppress the physical side of the response.

We are not advocating 'acting out' every impulse we feel. We strongly believe, however, that *combining* your awareness of the physical components of the stress response with your mature, rational, thinking side will allow you to make the most appropriate response and thereby reduce your stress. For example, the frustration of having your parking spot 'stolen' by a cheeky motorist may tempt you to act out by throttling them; fantasising about letting their tyres down during the five minutes it takes you to walk from your new spot fulfils both your anger and your need to do something physical.

AN ANCIENT RESPONSE TO MODERN LIFE

It makes sense to speculate that the stress response was designed for a life that was for the most part low in stimulation but punctuated by rare times when the fight or flight response was required to activate our systems. Running the body at a fast pace over long periods of time, such as when the adrenaline-based stress response goes on for too long, or is activated too often in response to low-scale situations, means that this survival mechanism can become extremely destructive. Chronic stress can lead to health breakdown.

We need to alternate periods of high stress with periods of rest and relaxation.

Stress and Strength

Sometimes the stress response can help people perform feats of strength or endurance they would not normally be capable of. This is termed 'hysterical strength'.

For example, a 16-year-old boy in Auckland was helping his father work on his car, which was jacked up on bricks. The unthinkable occurred, and the car slipped off the blocks, trapping the man underneath. The son seized the car and held it off his father long enough for others to drag the injured man free. This case of unusual strength was confirmed by police officers who attended the scene.

THE SEESAW LAW

If our system acted as it was meant to, then after each arousal (when the stress response is turned on) we would perform some *physical* activity, use all the energy and chemicals produced in our bodies and, providing we'd survived, we would rest until we felt 'back to normal'. We would have obeyed what we call the seesaw law of stress – UP, PHYSICAL ACTION, DOWN.

It follows that if there is no chance to rest or recover, then all the little hassles and stresses of the day can pile up, increasing our overall stress levels.

Stress is cumulative and builds upon all the other stresses.

That can be seen in the diagram on the next page. The seesaw law requires that we rest and recuperate following some effort or stressful exertion. If that opportunity doesn't arise, *or if there are multiple stressors that keep the stress response activated*, then the body must work harder to keep up a level of arousal to meet each 'threat'.

THE PHYSICAL STRESS REACTION

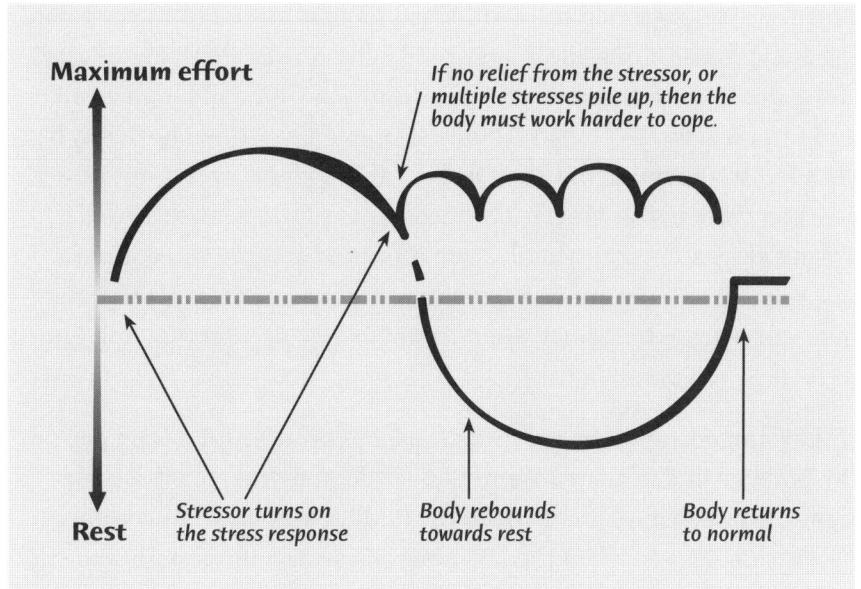

Under conditions of constant pressure or when we cannot attain relief, some researchers have speculated that the stress response becomes 'hyper-reactive'. This means that it becomes accustomed to firing all the time – almost as if we have formed a physical habit of responding to all situations as if they were stress situations.

One of the other consequences of chronic stress arousal is that as the body becomes used to operating closer to its alarm reaction all the time, our tolerance levels are reduced. People under constant stress do tend to be more irritable, jumpy, nervy or worrisome. The flip side of that coin is that it becomes much harder to relax, almost as if the body is on a semi-permanent war footing.

LONG-TERM STRESS

What we have described so far is the initial stage of the stress response, often called the *alarm phase*, which is designed to activate the body's resources. In this sense we are still 'wild' animals. If the threat continues, or if other threats arise, then the stress reaction keeps the body in a state of readiness.

However, if we are exposed to some stressors often enough, we get used to them. They no longer have the same impact on our system.

What happens if people are maintained under constant, high levels of stress for extended periods? Wars have provided 'natural laboratories' to observe what happens. The result seems to be a *potentiation* of the stress response, or a marked decrease in the stimulus required to set stress off. Thus we see soldiers suffer from stress-related syndromes like startle reflex, in which they jump, flinch or get a fright from sights or sounds that don't bother most other people, such as a car backfiring.

This was demonstrated to David when he first moved to the city and lived in a house alongside a busy road. The constant roaring of cars along the street was intrusive. The sound was especially loud at night, and for a few weeks he had trouble sleeping. Over time, however, he got used to the noise and slept better (although he swears not as well as when there is real quiet). This process works in reverse as well. Taking away a normal stimulus can also produce unwanted arousal: just watch a city person in a quiet country house ('Gee, it's so quiet here') or a cigarette addict when trying to give up ('Stop saying I'm irritable – I'm bloody not!')

If the demands upon us are numerous, or continue for a long period, the body begins to adapt. We no longer demonstrate the dramatic signs of the alarm phase. Instead the body settles down to coping as best it can. This is called the *resistance* phase, when our ability to cope will actually *increase*. (At last, you say, this is how stress is useful.) Stress of this kind allows us to burn the midnight oil and keep going beyond our normal limits. The body adjusts and starts operating in high gear.

This stage of the stress reaction consumes energy at a much faster rate than if we were relaxed or resting. In addition, the body produces higher levels of hormones and steroids (the natural equivalent of performance-enhancing drugs), which help it to repair itself quickly and keep going. We may feel that we are dealing with the situation well and may even feel pretty good. Nonetheless, our bodies are working much harder and cannot go on coping like this indefinitely. Unless we rest and recover, the cost to our system is quite high.

We pay that cost through, for example, increased susceptibility to illness because of a lowered immune response. We might also become short-tempered and irritable. Little things suddenly seem huge. Memory and concentration don't seem to be as good. Time is spent fixing mistakes that were made because we were 'multi-tasking' or trying to keep too many things on the go at once. We may withdraw or reduce time spent with friends and family. Ironically, we stop doing things that helped keep us well, such as exercise or regular meals, because it now seems to be 'too much hassle'.

The third stage of the stress response occurs when the body has used up all of its resources and has no more to give. This stage is called *exhaustion* and is sometimes marked by the re-emergence of some of the signs of the alarm phase. We will discuss this phase in more detail below.

None of these states is permanent, and it is timely to remember that the physical reactions we experience are normal. Learning skills of deep relaxation and specific ways to manage our physical reactions are vital stress management steps, and can be found from chapter 5 onwards in this book.

The Unconscious Stress Response
Since the stress response is preparing us for action in some way, it follows that stressed individuals will display signs of wanting to move or to act, such as being physically tense, or fidgeting and displaying nervous energy; or they will display signs of trying to *suppress* these mental and physical responses, as in rigidity, stiffness, sweating and so on. Very often we may not even be aware that we are feeling tense, especially if our circumstances won't allow us simply to up and leave. Some situations call for us to mask or hide our responses – such as in a dentist's waiting room when we try to hide our fear, or at a neighbour's when we feel really bored but don't want to offend them.

Research on the physical expression of emotion, carried out by Dr Paul Ekman, has revealed that we must work quite hard to continue to hide or suppress such feelings and emotions. One of his particular areas of interest is lying, and his studies asked the question: how well can humans lie? (It is believed some animals, especially chimpanzees, do this as well). He did find that some people can lie in ways that are essentially undetectable, but the number of people who can do this is not very high. In fact, in the majority of cases there are signs of *leakage* that show we cannot easily hide what it is that we feel strongly.

As an example of leakage, Dr Ekman described the case of a nurse who was filmed as she talked about how much she *liked* her supervisor, when in reality she strongly *disliked* her. Watching the movement of her hands, it was noticed that she often held her hands

Dr Paul Ekman is probably the world's foremost expert on body language, particularly of the face. Read *Unmasking the Face*, Paul Ekman and Wallace Friesen, New Jersey, Prentice-Hall.,1975

in fists – except for the middle finger on her right hand, which was extended in a well-known sign. The nurse was completely unaware of what she had been unconsciously saying about the supervisor.

Ekman's work clearly shows that while we may not recognise that we are ourselves under stress, friends, workmates or family may notice changes in mood, attitude or behaviour before we do. Our difficulty in recognising a problem may not simply reflect ignorance or bloody-mindedness either. Sometimes we are not psychologically ready or prepared to acknowledge that a problem exists, and unconsciously we may hope that it disappears before we have to deal with it. Alternatively, the problem may be so worrying or threatening to us that we are scared of what will happen if we confront it. Psychologically this is called 'denial' – the hope that if we don't acknowledge or recognise a problem, it won't be real.

A good example of this sort of denial occurs in a marriage, when one partner leaves the other to pursue an ongoing affair. Many people we have counselled denied that they noticed any changes in their partners, even when friends said things like, 'You know, I *thought* something was going on.' Acknowledging to ourselves that there are signs of strain in a relationship, then bringing such a threat into the open means many issues have to be confronted and the marriage itself may even be in question. Leaving things hidden, on the other hand, may be unconsciously stressful for the individual, but seemingly unthreatening to the marriage.

The best sign of stress: look for changes from a previous state. The second best sign of stress: losing our sense of humour!

If a person who is normally tolerant and sociable begins to snap and snarl, or seems to have no time for talking any more, it is a good bet they are under some kind of stress.

SIGNS OF STRESS

Each of us is unique in our responses to various stressors and events in our lives. We differ too in our genetic constitution, psychological make-up, physical attributes, social circumstances and available supports. All of these will impact on how we cope with and show signs of stress. Nevertheless, there are some reliable indicators that tell us if we, or someone we know, is under some sort of pressure.

Bear in mind that these are simply indicators of generalised distress, not of any specific ailment or disorder. Try to be aware of the underlying message of the stress response: it is a call to action in some way.

Try this exercise and see how many of these apply to you now.

PHYSICAL SIGNS OF STRESS

Tiredness, fatigue	
Difficulty catching breath, frequent deep sighing, shallow, rapid breaths	
Increased perspiration - especially on the hands, feet and face	
Cold hands (because the blood moves towards the body under stress)	
Muscular tension. Others will see clenched or jutting jaw, frowning, stiff neck, shoulders carried high, frequent fidgety movement, difficulty keeping still, wringing of the hands	
Grinding teeth, sore muscles, tight stomach	
Frequent urge to urinate	
Increased illness - especially colds that won't go, small rashes	
Headaches, migraines, tinnitus	
Dry mouth, difficulty swallowing (because saliva dries up under stress)	
Diarrhoea and stomach upsets, heartburn	
Easily startled, jumpy, nervous, anxious	
Trembling or shaking	
Significant weight change (without dieting)	

BEHAVIOURAL AND PERFORMANCE SIGNS OF STRESS

Difficulty sleeping; sleep not restorative	
Changes in appearance; slippage in personal standards	
Routines break down; apathy and indifference	
Reduced activity levels; a tendency to 'cruise' or 'blob out'	
Mental disorganisation, difficulty concentrating, forgetting things	
Multi-tasking inefficiently; too many things on the go	
Missing deadlines, meetings, appointments (not just very occasionally)	
Work piles up; quality breaks down	
Avoidance of certain situations or people	
Calls not returned	
Absences; increased sick days	
Increased use of alcohol, drugs (including pain killers), overeating, partying	

RELATIONSHIP AND EMOTIONAL SIGNS OF STRESS

Cynical, hostile or rigid attitudes to work or other circumstances	
Hardening of stances on touchy issues	
Reduced tolerance; inability to see both sides of an issue; grumpy with children or partner	
Marked mood swings or changes	
Unhappiness with life; finding fault, irrational blaming	
Powerful emotions - distress, anger, fear - closer to the surface	
Withdrawal from friends, lovers	
Avoidance of social situations and commitments	
Sexual appetite falls away	
Able to talk only about 'problems'	

Don't wait to be told!

Our rule of thumb is that if you have 7–10 of these signs (or more), and they persist for two weeks, then you need to take action (and you know that you were right to read this book).

Each person will react and respond to stress in different ways. Don't wait until your body begins to break down and develop illnesses. Recognise the signs of tension and upset in yourself, and use them as an early-warning system. Act to improve your well-being.

Some of these signs may be caused by stress, but they may also be the result of other factors, including illness. It pays to have an examination by a qualified medical practitioner to exclude physical illness.

CHAPTER 3

The health consequences of stress

This chapter examines the relationship between stress, our health and behaviour. Is it true that stress actually causes heart attacks? Top New Zealand health psychology researcher Dr Keith Petrie spoke to a large group of heart patients in Auckland Hospital after their attacks and found that the majority *believed* that stress was the major cause of their coronary. Is stress implicated in cancer? An increasing body of evidence suggests that it may be, in part because of research that links high stress levels with reduced immune function, and also because of the identification of a 'cancer-prone personality' profile.

But is there a causal link between stress and disease? We say there isn't, although stress unquestionably *contributes* to disease and our ability to cope or heal.

Reading this article from Wellington's *Dominion* newspaper in November 1993, one could reasonably decide that overwork leads to the sudden death syndrome identified in Japan as 'kiroshi'.

> For the second time in a month a Japanese company has agreed to pay compensation to relatives of an employee who died of overwork. Tsubakimoto Precision Products pledged 50 million yen (NZ$812,500) in an out-of-court settlement to the family of Satoru Hiraoka, who died of heart failure in

> 1988 at the age of 48, a company spokesman said yesterday. The Osaka ball bearings manufacturer also apologised for not being considerate enough of Mr Hiraoka's health conditions. His family said he worked an average of 71 hours a week and died after working for 51 straight days.

We are sure you'll agree that 51 straight days of work is excessive. 'Kiroshi' or death through overwork appears to be the end result of the stressful lifestyle lived by the 'salarymen', the Japanese middle managers and office workers who are bound by traditions and strong norms to work long hours. But many other factors contribute to the kiroshi syndrome, aside from overwork. Work cultures that encourage persistently long hours, or relentless pressure for long periods without breaks, may cause stress. In Japan it is socially embarrassing, for example, to be the first to leave work at night. Other expected behaviours in Japanese organisations include heavy drinking with work colleagues, and unswerving loyalty to the company, even at the expense of family and personal life. Japanese men are also known to smoke heavily. In short, there are likely to have been many factors contributing to this man's death – although overwork is undoubtedly one of them.

It is interesting that there is no comparable term to kiroshi in English, although the concept is certainly alive and well, so to speak, in many organisations. A hospital ward we know of has a cultural norm that frowns on people taking their lunch break. Law firms are well known for 'unwritten rules' concerning the hours junior lawyers must work, and woe betide the junior who leaves before his or her senior partner.

What cultural messages exist in your working environment concerning stress and effort?

It makes sense to believe that stress is intimately related to health. The stress response is a *generalised physical reaction* to nearly any demand or challenge that we are presented with. This response was designed to prepare the body for dealing with life-or-death threats, and also to arouse and sustain the body for only relatively short bursts of action. Unfortunately, stress is triggered in other ways as well. Thoughts and memories can activate it, as can threats to our social, economic and personal esteem. (See chapter 2 for more details on the physiology of stress, and chapter 5 for how thinking impacts on stress.) It is also known that constant stressors or extremely high levels of stress for long periods have an impact on our mental and physical well-being.

However, there is absolutely no reason to believe that being stressed is a sure-fire route to illness, let alone death. While the kiroshi deaths in Japan are sad and dramatic, what about the millions of other Japanese salarymen who survive and cope (although it doesn't sound like much of a life)? And for that matter, what of the people in milk-bars and corner shops who also work long seven-day weeks without let-up, but who remain well and even enjoy what they do?

The stress response is a normal response in the body. Feeling stressed is unpleasant, but first and foremost it is a sign to us that something in our life is causing us distress. In that sense it is a powerful ally. To respond to bad feelings by taking a painkiller, drinking alcohol or using other methods of simply blocking them out is missing the point.

Stress is a call to change something, and we ignore it at our peril.

But the key point is that we must understand such bad feelings in their context. Negative health effects are going to result only from long periods of sustained stress, especially if we maintain a generally unhealthy lifestyle by smoking or drinking too much or eating poorly, and if we tend to suppress negative emotions.

ILLNESS IS NOT AN INEVITABLE OUTCOME OF STRESS

Life events impact on how we view the event, how we cope with it and the ways we manage our lives. It is the sum of these factors that creates the conditions in which illness may occur. And even then we are not immune, as reactions from others to the illness, or the way we act ourselves, will also impinge on our stress levels. It is not a simple relationship!

The diagram below shows the many factors that impinge on health.

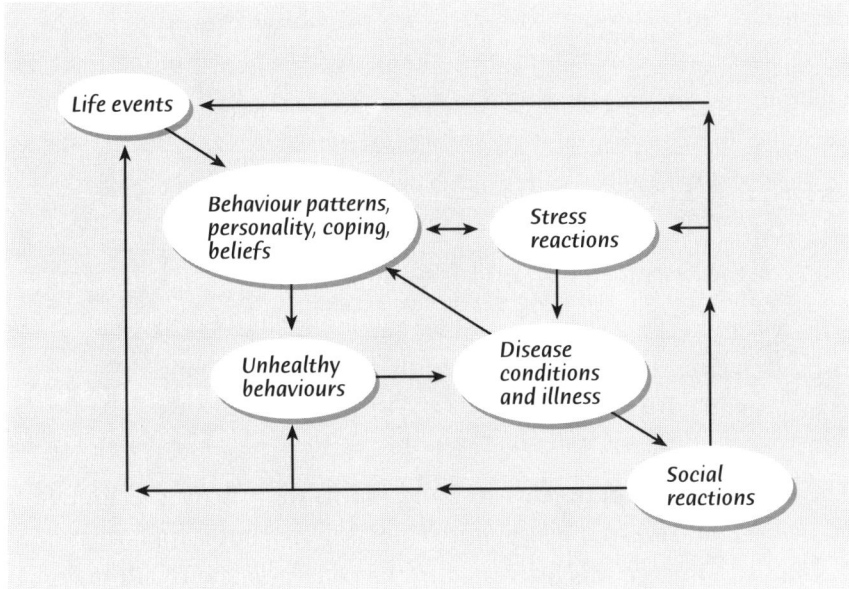

Although the diagram looks complex, the ideas it contains apply easily to the real world. A client of ours had recently suffered the death of her husband (a life event). Left with three young children, her daily life had to change markedly in order to manage the family. She also grieved terribly for her husband (a stress reaction). To make matters worse, without her husband's income she could no longer afford to remain in her house and the family moved to damp, uncongenial rented accommodation. She took to smoking again, an unhealthy behaviour that she said helped her cope. The combination of her grief, the extra load she carried, smoking and poor housing led to her suffering serious bronchitis and eventually pneumonia. (This was about the lowest point for our client – the story eventually had a happier outcome.)

> An interesting book by James Lynch examined whether loneliness, bereavement and divorce affect heart disease. He found, for example, that the death rate from coronary heart disease was about two times higher among divorced people compared to married couples. Among widowed people and singles, the rate was about one and a half times greater.
>
> Lynch observed that human contact has a positive impact on the actual heart beats of people in coronary care units, and that recovery time is faster for those with significant social supports.
>
> Other research confirms his results – and why not, when we use terms like *heartsick*, *heartbroken* and *heartache*? In the words of the song, 'Only love can mend a broken heart'.

James Lynch, *The Broken Heart*, New York, Basic Books, 1977

The first clear link between stress and illness was discovered after many years of research by scientist Hans Selye (whose work we noted in chapter 1). Selye was interested in the consequences of adrenaline in the body and he spent years causing stress in rats by pulling on their tails and allowing them no relief (rats hate this). Examining the rats after death, he discovered that they had greatly enlarged adrenal glands, shrinkage of other organs, and ulcers in the stomach and intestines. Such findings showed graphically that many of the body's various systems and organs become involved when the stress response is triggered.

So Selye demonstrated that the first way that stress can lead to illness is *through general wear and tear.* The body expends energy to maintain high levels of arousal, and the damage arises from remaining in an aroused state for a long period of time. Although the evidence implicates many factors in the development of stress-related diseases, negative emotional states associated with stress also play their part.

The other striking research that linked social stress and illness came from the work of two United States Navy doctors, Holmes and Rahe. They noticed when families transferred to a new naval base that they tended to have more visits to the health centre than did staff who had been there for a year or more. Fascinated, they did a lot of research in the 1960s which showed that there was indeed a relationship between social stress and the *likelihood* of illness. Note that this isn't a causal link; rather it suggests that if we have experienced a large number of events requiring some social readjustment, then our risk of illness is significantly raised, at least compared to someone whose life is more settled. Even more fascinating, these don't even have to be *negative* events for the relationship to hold true.

Unfortunately, this research came to be misunderstood as scientists overemphasised the relationship between life events and illness, to the point that it was assumed that a large number of life events would cause illness. Not true! Not everyone who has a stressful period in their lives goes on to suffer.

Ensuing research has gone on to implicate stress as a *contributing factor* in a number of illnesses. We have listed out a few specific diseases and conditions which have been very well researched and demonstrated to have a link with stress. Most of them seem pretty logical when we understand the physiology of the stress response.

Holmes & Rahe, The Social Readjustment Rating Scale, Journal of Psychosomatic Research, 1967, 11, 213-218.

Physical diseases linked to stress and personality variables	Method of action
• coronary heart disease	*raises blood pressure, blocks arteries, increases workload*
• asthma	*may predispose to attacks, induces spasm of bronchi*
• arthritis	*impacts immune system*
• headache	*tension, blood pressure*
• muscular disorders	*tension*
• depression	*feelings of helplessness, hopelessness, disorganised thinking, changed neurotransmitter function*
• common cold	*impacts immune response*

Note, however, that stress is unlikely to be the only cause of an illness. It is far more likely that stress plays a 'step-in' role that makes our susceptibility to illness greater, or our defence (immune) system weaker. Cigarette smoking, genetic make-up, diet and other factors play major roles. Stress is unlikely to be the only factor.

The relationship between stress and the common cold was investigated in a very good study by three researchers, led by Sheldon Cohen. This team locked up 400 volunteers (not all at once) in a sealed environment. They screened them all for prior illness and then gave them nose drops containing one of several types of cold germs and viruses. Then the researchers sat back and let nature take its course.

Sheldon Cohen, D. Tyrell & A. Smith, 'Psychological stress and susceptibility to the common cold', New England Journal of Medicine, 1991, pp. 606-12.

This study was extremely well conducted. The subjects completed many physical and psychological tests before, during and after the study. The researchers even counted the number of tissues used by each subject (that is certainly above and beyond the call of duty!). The results showed that there was a positive relationship between the amount of psychological stress reported and whether the subjects got a cold. At the higher levels of stress, people were more likely to become sick; this related directly to the body's ability to fight infection. Cohen and his colleagues elegantly confirmed many previous findings that stress has a weakening effect on the immune system.

There are a wealth of studies demonstrating that stress can impact on a wide range of conditions, including depression, suicide, anorexia, psychiatric illness, diabetes, alcoholism, accidents, back pain, tinnitus, blurred vision, kidney disease, skin rashes, psoriasis, multiple sclerosis, cancer, spastic colon, impotence, vaginismus and even premature ejaculation.

Recent evidence seems to suggest that people of certain personality dispositions may be sensitised to stress and over-react to seemingly trivial situations. This line of research proposes that the stress response behaves like an allergy, becoming increasingly sensitive to the presence of events that trigger the flood of responses that ought to be reserved for life-threatening situations.

PERSONALITY AND STRESS

One of the most studied personality types in which stress can impact on heart disease is the Type A personality pattern. In the 1950s two American cardiologists called Friedman and Rosenman, noticed a relationship between heart disease and behaviour. Legend has it that when an upholsterer arrived to fix some chairs in their offices, he asked what kind of doctors they were, because only the fronts of the chairs were worn out. Heart patients, it seemed, sat only on the fronts of the chairs!

The cardiologists went on to describe a behaviour pattern that is called Type A. Type A individuals are characterised by their sense of time pressure, of taking life seriously, and by being competitive, impatient, perfectionist, compulsive and tense. The other defining characteristic is a repressed hostility or suppressed negative emotions (being annoyed).

We have observed that many organisations value and reward such behaviours. Type A individuals often do well in working life. Indeed in some industries (such as advertising or management consulting) people displaying Type A behaviour would seem to prevail.

Sadly, Type A characteristics, and particularly hostility, are extremely good predictors of heart disease – indeed as good as smoking, high blood pressure or genetic history! The mechanism by which this operates is not entirely clear, but in responding to stress Type A men tend to produce higher levels of chemicals that have an effect on the heart and on the absorption of fats. It is reasonable to assume that this may be the way stress impacts on heart disease.

One of the fathers of Type A research, H.M. Friedman, has written a good general guide to health psychology. H.M. Friedmann & M.R. DiMatteo, *Health Psychology*, Boston, Prentice Hall, 1989.

So stress *does* affect our health. And if it affects our health, then it must be bad, right? What do you do about it?

Watch out for that disease!
Avoid salt!
Don't eat fats!
Don't get angry!
Don't work too hard!

Rubbish! Take all the advice on offer, and the safest way to avoid stress would be to lock ourselves in a room and never come out!

In chapter 5 we will examine the opposite notion to all the hype and fear messages; that despite all manner of awful situations and stressors, *most people cope well most of the time.* Surely it makes more sense to think about the things that promote a good all-round level of coping?

As much as stress impacts on our health and immune systems, there are few situations in modern life for which stress is an essential survival response. That means that such stress as we feel is a product of how we mentally view events or react to them – a thought which opens up the possibility that we have just as much power to influence our responses *in positive ways.* In the next chapter we will explore more deeply how our view of the world and our thoughts can affect stress.

CHAPTER 4

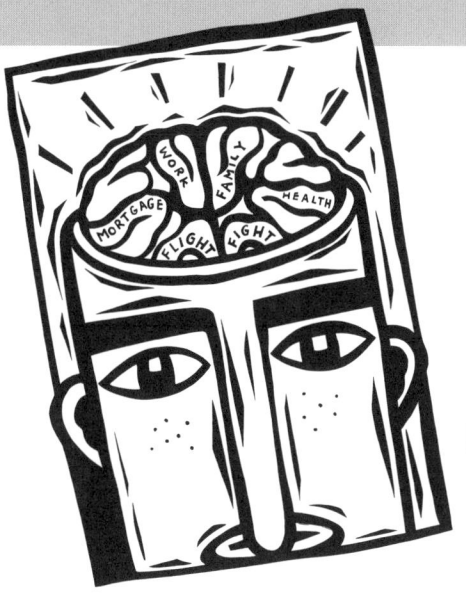

Stress and the brain

While writing this chapter, David was listening to a discussion on the radio about the effects of mortgage interest rate increases. On the rise again! The radio host seemed to be concerned about the impact of this on people's lives. They would be worried, she noted, because there seemed to be so little *certainty* in people's expectations – the rates may even go higher.

As he listened David found himself feeling worried too. He tried to do the calculation of what a 2% rise in his mortgage would translate into (never a good idea for someone so mathematically challenged). He began to estimate the flow-on effects, and his stomach began to tighten as he foresaw less money to spend on the things he wanted, curtailed holidays and arguments with his spouse over the budget. He even had a mental picture of the bank repossessing the house if he couldn't meet the payments.

Then the radio host moved on! She just changed the subject, played a Billie Holiday song ('Gloomy Sunday') and started talking about a forest park walk. What about the interest rate rises? What about us worried mortgage holders?

Unwittingly David had fallen into the trap of *catastrophising*. The trap involves losing perspective, getting lost in the minutiae of a problem or issue and reacting as if this hassle, this problem, is the biggest thing in the world. Notice that it was his thoughts alone that caused him to worry and become stressed, because in reality the rate rise had not yet occurred.

The incredible power our minds have to affect our physical responses is now a commonplace notion, and one harnessed by professional athletes to improve their physical performance. Does it also hold that the reverse is true and that physical reactions can affect our thinking?

An experiment done many years ago investigated the way stress impacts on thinking and information processing. (If the experiment now seems a bit 'shocking', consider that modern ethical procedures mean it would be very unlikely to get approval today.)

J. Tanner, *Stress and Psychiatric Disorder*, Oxford, Basil, Blackwell & Mott, 1960

Imagine a specially prepared room which has 11 exit doors, each of a different colour. The floor is a metal grid, which can be electrified. Your job, once inside the room, is to get out again as fast as you can – a desirable state of affairs, because you will be in there without your shoes and socks, getting electric shocks from the floor!

There is one rule that you need to remember, however: *only one door will open, and any door you escaped from (say the red door) will not open to you again.*

The first time you enter the room the level of current in the floor is very low, though still unpleasant. How will you behave?

As you get put back into the room after each successful escape, the level of current will increase, until it becomes painful. How will you behave now? Has your behaviour changed in any way?

History doesn't tell us what became of the brave subjects in this study. The results were dramatic, however.

Under low shock conditions the behaviour of the subjects was observed to be controlled and rational. They wasted no time in finding the door through a systematic search and exiting fast.

As shock increased, however, the rational problem-solving behaviour disappeared, to be replaced with frantic, almost random rushing around, with time being wasted and no evidence of careful thought.

When the shock reached a certain critical level of pain, the behaviour of the subjects deteriorated entirely, leading them to attempt to exit *the door they escaped from last time,* even though they knew 'rationally' that this strategy wouldn't work. In their desperation and distress they 'reverted' to old knowledge as a means of coping.

We think that this experiment, although drastic, demonstrates the way in which stress strongly affects thinking – it effectively shuts off our ability to behave thoughtfully, carefully and rationally.

One of the most basic consequences of stress is the change in the manner, focus and level of our thinking. This occurs because there exists more than one information-processing route in the brain.

THINKING ABOUT THE BRAIN

Let's briefly digress to talk about the brain. Brains are not a solid lump of processing tissue. They have slowly changed and developed over millions of years of evolution, with little lumps and accretions adding to the specialised thinking power of humans.

In the brain the *cortex* is thought of as supplying the rational, abstract and planned part of our thinking and corresponds to the wrinkly outer layer of the brain. In evolutionary terms it is quite a recent development, although it has been with us for many thousands of years. This part of the brain processes information at a higher level, in that it is able to construct alternative scenarios, imagine the future, collate information from the past and predict responses. Without the cortex we perhaps wouldn't have architecture, music, mathematics, cars, jobs or systems of government. It is the part of the brain most readily associated with what we call our 'consciousness': it is where we are aware of ourselves and our own actions: 'Ah yes, I can see that if I continue to drive at 160 kph through this heavily built-up town, my chances of being nabbed by the law are quite high. That would lead to a court appearance, a fine, loss of my licence and considerable social embarrassment, not to mention the restriction of opportunity to take my planned driving holiday. I'll slow down.'

Deeper in the brain, under the layer of the cortex, we also have an older, more 'primitive' information-passing system which works in parallel to our normal thought processing. Operating through the limbic system and a part of the brain called the *amygdala*, it processes information at a lower, more emotional and action-oriented level. This is the part of the brain referred to in chapter 2 when we described the fight or flight response.

This system is thought to be heavily involved in the generation of emotions. In conjunction with another part of the inner brain called the *hypothalamus*, it is charged with processing and regulating the myriad of information that is generally unconscious, and it modifies such things as temperature, hormone production, heart rate, sweating and so on. A moment's thought will make it clear that most of the time we don't consciously think about any of these processes, relying instead on some unknown part of the brain to do it for us.

The fundamental nature of this system is that it deals with information in a fast, action-based manner. Researchers speculate that it responds to anything vaguely related to a threat by firing the stress reaction.

You might think of it as a 'quick and dirty' response trigger – so fast in fact, that it may start an emotional response before we completely recognise what we are reacting to! You can observe it in yourself when a sudden movement, or seeing something you *thought* was dangerous, produces a 'shock' or caused you to jump.

For example, a patient at our stress clinic walked into a room and suddenly screamed, sending half the other people there running in panic too. But from what? The screaming woman (once she stopped) was sheepish as she explained that she thought the coil of video cable she had glimpsed in the dim corner was a snake. A snake? There aren't any snakes in New Zealand! Her brain had interpreted the coil as *possibly* a snake and had triggered the fight or flight response, before she consciously processed the image as a coil of cable.

That example shows that the limbic system is *non-selective*, reacting just as fast to imagined or dimly perceived threats as to real ones. Simply imagining something upsetting or worrying can result in an emotional reaction and the activation of the body.

Another automatic response acts to calm down and control such reactions once we send a signal that everything is all right, and may operate most of the time without our being consciously aware of it. Importantly, however, this calming response is set up to defer to the arousal one, which makes great sense in the many animal species which live in a state of constant watchfulness in order to avoid ending up as someone's lunch. Humans, on the other hand, rarely need it.

Many of the negative aspects of stress result from the brain's hard-wired tendency to give precedence to *runaway fear*. This changes both what we pay attention to and the speed of our thinking, demanding that we focus on threats and concerns.

In firefighting circles the expression 'head off, cabbage on' is used to describe the reactions of some firefighters when they panic. One story related to us by an Australian firefighter is of a commander who arrived at a huge, out-of-control house fire. Commanders are meant to take control at the scene and direct resources. However, this man leapt from his vehicle and ran quickly, but aimlessly, around and around the fire engine, shouting, 'Where's the hose! Where's the hose!'

He provides us with a good example of psychological overload. Overload can produce seemingly bizarre behaviour which approximates what a person is meant to do, exactly as described in the 11 doors experiment. The fire commander was in the grip of the flight part of the stress response but acting without useful cognitive (thinking) control or direction. In our experience, this mostly results from high levels of stress in more than just the work-related aspects of life.

This is why so much time is spent in routine drills and training exercises for soldiers, police personnel and others whose lives may depend on their *reacting* in predictable and useful ways during extreme stress. The drills must replace the automatic and chaotic fear responses with other, deeply ingrained habits of behaving in an orderly and reliable way.

AN OVER-USED STRESS RESPONSE

There is some recent evidence to suggest that many stressful episodes, or stress without relief, actually increases the effects and reaction times of the brain's stress response, in much the same way that an allergy sensitises hay-fever sufferers. Small frustrations lead to intense responses; the sufferer experiences ongoing irritability or anxiety, and usually a pervasive feeling of tiredness. No wonder. Maintaining the body in a such constant state of arousal saps the energy and is ultimately harmful.

Low-Level Thinking

Remember that the stress response is non-selective and treats most information passed to it as if it were real. Imagine this scenario:

You are sitting at your desk and glance casually at the clock. Suddenly you realise it's 2.15! You had a meeting with your boss and her manager at 2.00! Oh no! You leap to your feet, spilling some papers to the floor. What do you need? What will they be saying? They're bound to be really mad. Damn! You can't find the file. Where is it? Did someone else have it? Oh please be there. Better get your coat. (Now the coat won't go on!) What was it you rehearsed the other day? 'There is a need to develop a strong…? Oh, no! Where on earth is the file, the file, the file? Is this a conspiracy?!

This is an example of what we call low-level thinking. In it we detect shades of the behaviour seen in the volunteers in the 11-doored room: the mindless rushing and action-at-all-costs approach. Low-level thinking emerges under stress and is characterised by being *reactive, emotional, spur-of-the-moment, unplanned and irrational*. If this has ever happened to you, then you will understand how the feedback part of the loop operates, making the experience of rushing and panic stressful in itself. The more worked up you become, the harder it is to think clearly and to co-ordinate your actions.

We summarise the differences between low-level thinking and clear thinking below:

High-level thinking (CORTEX)	Low-level thinking (LIMBIC)
rational	*gut level*
analytical	*spontaneous*
logical	*instinctive*
critical	*reactionary*
thoughtful	*not data based*
unemotional	*rash*
careful	*hurried*
thought through	*emotive*
balanced	

Can you think of times you have detected these differences in your thoughts? When did the cortex thinking occur? When were your thoughts dominated by limbic thinking (probably not a time of which you were so proud)?

Stress exists to sharpen the focus of attention when there is a clear and present danger. But as we saw in the example above, the basic 'call to action' command can seem to trip us up. This effect seems particularly pronounced when we are trying to juggle many tasks, worries or deadlines in our minds at the same time.

The fact that stress influences thinking and thinking influences stress actually opens up many chances to modify and manage our stress reactions. Let's look at one way people naturally do this, all in the name of fun.

Why Bungy Jumping is all in the Mind

People who have completed a bungy jump report feeling incredibly proud (justifiably, we think!). When they make it down, they are literally jumping with excitement. In their euphoria, they feel they have conquered some primitive fear or have even won something.

Jubilation is a wonderful feeling: you can see it in their eyes, which are wide with excitement, their flushed cheeks, their shaky voices and rushed speech.

But hang on a minute. Only moments before, at the top of the bungy platform, we saw quite the opposite. Most people describe those moments on the edge of a platform 100 metres from the ground as *sheer naked terror*. We would have seen they were quaking with fear, with their hearts beating wildly, stomachs doing flip-flops, eyes wide with terror, clearly possessed of a strong urge to get out of there.

And why? Because deep in the primitive part of their brain is the certainty that if they leap 100 metres headfirst to the ground they are going to die, of course! The message goes out to activate all systems: prepare for some heavy-duty escape action, activate the 'flee' part of the fight or flight response, and drop the lifeboats.

An old adage says 'whatever doesn't kill you makes you stronger', a sentiment we seem to instinctively grasp only after a bungy-jump is over.

Yet the majority of people (who pay upwards of $80 for this experience) don't flee. Their cortex, that rational part of them, holds them on the edge when their every instinct is to escape. 'Trust me,' says the cortex, 'I know what I am doing. The rubber band tied to our legs is going to save us. Hundreds of people have done it. I can do it! You'll embarrass us if you back down now. Besides, this is fun, isn't it?'

We mentally *label* this experience fun. By silently talking to ourselves, we turn the naked terror into excitement or exhilaration and a sense of triumph.

The emotional sensations associated with our feelings and basic needs are probably generated in the limbic system. In her delightful book, New Zealand psychologist Margit Brew describes what happens when we play mind games with ourselves:

Margit Brew, Stress and Distress, Auckland, Methuen, 1982.

> *A strong difference ... between what the body wants and what the mind wants leads to illness. Imagine for instance that your nephew comes to stay with you. There are many things you resent about him. You resent his looks, his voice and his manners. In fact, you can't stand him. But your cerebral cortex wants to be nice, it rationalises that you should be nice because... it is proper to be courteous and*

kind to relatives, especially as he is the child of your favourite brother with whom you do not want to fall out. Your continuous unresolved feeling of resentment means that the thalamus is thwarted... and when this happens scrambled messages are sent to the body... because you have been too busy being nice to the world and not heeding the messages of your body.

In the scientific world it is generally held that humans are the only species able to alter our thalamic response – our physical reactions, attitudes, beliefs and even behaviour – just through *thinking*. The evidence of our ability to do this exists whenever we get happy or angry or sad when thinking about another person, or ride a rollercoaster for the *joy* of it. It is evident whenever we watch a horror movie because 'we love being terrified'.

The Revenge of the Cows

Unfortunately, the same ability to comment on our own thoughts and behaviour can work the other way and become a liability. We worry about events *that haven't even occurred* and imagine how they will turn out. Psychologists have a special word for worry: *rumination*, that comes from the same root word in Latin as ruminant, describing the family of animals to which cows belong. Cows have this name because they chew their cud, bringing back food material to chew it over some more and, as they do so, looking for all the world as if they are gently pondering higher thoughts. Humans ruminate by bringing unfinished psychological material back to our conscious minds and then pondering the ins and outs, pros and cons. But unlike cows who produce something useful at the end (milk), we end up with little to show for our efforts but feelings of anxiety, indecision and doubts.

The way humans usually ruminate is by running through different scenarios in our minds. Consider the following situation in which two people experience exactly the same event, but end up reacting and feeling completely differently:

Two office workers arrive back at their desks after lunch to find notes from the chief executive (whom they rarely see) that simply say, 'See me on your return'. Michael immediately feels a cold guilt and runs through all the things that he may have done wrong, dreading the encounter and wondering if he is about to be sacked. Not surprisingly, he feels anxious, unhappy and tense, though nothing has happened yet!

Michelle also wonders what the chief executive wants, but feels more excited than nervous. Asking herself whether this is an invitation to the special project she's heard about, or a move or even a promotion, she looks forward to the meeting with a sense of expectation.

The only difference between the two people is the way in which they deal with the ambiguous note in their minds. For Michael, running through disaster scenarios produces unhappiness, whereas Michelle leaves open the possibility of a positive outcome, and consequently manages to attend the meeting with an optimistic outlook. Michelle also saves herself a lot of needless worry and stress by keeping her body calm and relaxed. By balancing the stress seesaw, she prevents the runaway reaction that leads to needless fear or anxiety.

We have observed through our work that people who complain of stress often have a style of thinking that is like Michael's. They tend to worry a lot about bad things that have yet to happen, and either lean towards magnifying the negative possibilities of a situation or see it in black-and-white terms: it's either all bad or all good. This is an open invitation for the stress response to gear up to meet this anticipated 'disaster'.

Psychologists have labelled the type of stress that this engenders *anticipatory stress.* As the name suggests, it arises because the brain has the facility to imagine a whole range of scenarios, both good and not-so-good. The possibilities we worry about turn on the stress response just as effectively as real situations do. Equally, sending conscious messages of calm and of control has the effect of toning down the stress response.

That is an incredibly powerful idea. It means that we balance on the line between terror and excitement, overload and challenge, and that the ability to determine which side of the line we fall on is entirely up to us. The way we view the world, talk to ourselves and judge our experiences is all in our heads.

For example, in the middle of a really scary movie, one watcher will sometimes 'step back', evaluate and then modify their feelings and thoughts with a comment like: 'I'm really sucked into this film. I'm feeling absolutely terrified. I'm going to concentrate on imagining the camera and lights in front of the vampire, and all the make-up they must be wearing, and that will calm me down.'

The significance of these concepts lies in the oft-repeated phrase 'stressing out about stress', something we will look at again in chapter 5.

TWO SIDES OF THE SAME COIN

While we have explored the idea that the stress response is a physically based defence mechanism to arouse the body and prepare it for action, we need to consider the other side of the coin – the manner in which the brain and body work to turn off the stress response and calm the body again. It is termed the relaxation response, and is mediated through the *parasympathetic nervous system.*

The parasympathetic nervous system operates through many of the same brain pathways as the arousal (stress) one, but acts as a foil for it, rather like the other end of a seesaw. When the stress response is in ascendancy, the parasympathetic system is down, or non-operational. When the stress response is no longer needed, then the parasympathetic system is in control, unwinding the effects of the stress response. Blood pressure drops and the heart rate slows, breathing slows and becomes deeper, muscle tone becomes relaxed, digestion is stimulated and a sense of relaxation steals through the body. The parasympathetic message is: 'It's okay, relax, recuperate.'

The relaxation response enables the body to slow down and rest from the effects of the stress reaction. Like the stress response, it is also heavily influenced by thoughts and feelings. In his influential book *The Relaxation Response,* Dr Herbert Benson theorised that learning to influence the parasympathetic response directly is possible through specific techniques. He makes the point that it is not a matter of simply sitting or lying down quietly; it requires a passive attitude and a sense of peace with the world. Here again we can see the importance of attitude and thinking in modifying our physical state.

This is a fantastic book. Herbert Benson, *The Relaxation Response*. New York, Wm Morrow & Co, 1975.

There is little real reason to fear stress when we realise that we have a built in stress-reduction device that responds to our mental commands and images. Learning to access it while managing other stressors is the simple art of stress management. Truly there is no real distinction between mind and body.

CHAPTER 5

Stress and your approach to life

In the previous chapters we saw that stress is a built-in response that causes us trouble by being triggered too frequently. It also has the unfortunate knack of firing as a result of the nature and style of our thoughts. We have arranged the rest of the book to emphasise these points. This chapter and chapters 6 and 7 all concentrate on *long-term* stress management, while the remainder of the book deals with *stress reduction* techniques. We believe this to be an important distinction. Reducing stress may help you to cope in the short term, but we would argue that feeling stressed is symptomatic of a life out of balance, and redressing that is a considerably more important task.

This simple message often seems to be the one people are least amenable to hearing. Taking time to reflect and consider whether we are enjoying our everyday relationships, work, and recreational and physical aspects of our life is a *long-term project* that necessarily means changing our fundamental approaches to life. While this may seem a dour message, consider that if you have any sense that life ought to be enjoyable, the question to reflect on might be: 'What do I need to do to feel more relaxed/peaceful/happy/fulfilled and so on?' The next three chapters provide our best response to achieving a life free from the *negative effects* of stress – not free from stress itself.

STOP THAT!

Recently we watched a well-known media personality on a television health and lifestyle programme describing her approach to health:

> *Well, I watch my diet carefully. I don't eat meat, I avoid any cholesterol and fats and I have completely cut salt out of my diet too. I try to avoid sugar if I can, although I have a real sweet tooth. I don't drink any alcohol any more and, you know, I don't let people get to me because anger is a really wasted emotion.*

We heard this person telling herself 'Don't, don't, don't!' What sort of life is that?

She epitomises what we have called the *stop that* approach to stress management. It says, in effect, that avoiding stress, or not having an illness, or not feeling run-down is the same as saying you are happy or healthy. We say, yes, cutting down on, say, fats and sugars *is* important for health, but remember not to cut out the enjoyment and joys from life too.

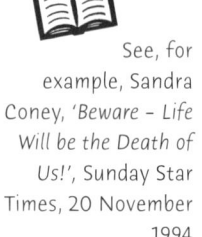
See, for example, Sandra Coney, 'Beware – Life Will be the Death of Us!', Sunday Star Times, 20 November 1994

New Zealand health activist and commentator Sandra Coney believes that there exists a 'health mafia' which seems to want to *terrify* us into paying attention to any sign that we are unwell. She suggests that we should bear in mind the powerful economic interests behind the promotion of messages that we should medicate ourselves to stay well and advertising that would have us believe that to exist in anything other than a state of perfect grace is unacceptable.

Our colleagues Keith Petrie and Jamie Pennebaker have likewise identified this trend and called it a 'puritan health ethic'. They believe that a strong attention to remaining in perfect health at all times may lead to people having a preoccupation with the absence of physical illness or imperfection. This thinking may paradoxically cause us to become 'sick with worry' about health concerns.

Edward Shorter tells how descriptions of vague symptoms may even get turned into 'diseases of fashion'. He reported one 1985 study of a group of Americans suffering from 'environmental hypersensitivity', a condition that had symptoms like tiredness, aching muscles, depression, digestive upset, dizziness and poor concentration. One year later the majority of these sufferers had changed their diagnosis to 'yeast allergy', a new condition which had been heavily publicised through popular media. The next year the researchers found that the diagnosis had changed again, this time to Epstein-Barr virus (a usually benign virus that exists in most humans, but which had been 'hyped' in the press). Shorter concluded, 'These patients are at high risk for acquiring diagnoses that are popularised in the media'. He maintained that modern western life has seen the demise of commonsense 'folk knowledge' about health and illness. Instead, individuals are bombarded by every 'new medical finding' on television and in print. People today, he said, are excessively 'sensitive to the signals their bodies give... they have acquired the unshakeable belief their symptoms represent a particular disease'.

Edward Shorter, From Paralysis to Fatigue: A History of Psychosomatic Illness in the Modern Era, New York, The Free Press, 1992.

The 'stop that' mentality is a bit silly for another reason: stress itself doesn't seem to function in a predictable way. The causes of our own distress are not always clear, and stress seems to affect different people in different ways. In fact many people report that stress makes them feel good or work better. Some people have had horrendous life experiences, smoke heavily and drink alcohol to excess all their lives, and yet have a happy, productive and more or less healthy existence until their old age.

Obviously stress is responsive to a number of factors, and applying the same stress-beating formula to all people seems to miss the point.

We strongly believe this points to a completely different way of thinking about stress. The most interesting thing about stress should not be the fact that people are exhausted or made ill by stress (they are – see chapter 3), but just the opposite idea: many of us cope pretty well most of the time, despite all manner of problems and hassles and troubles. Some individuals cope excellently all their lives *no matter what awful things happen*. What is their secret? What do they do that helps them enjoy life?

We will examine a few researchers who have taken time to try to understand what keeps people healthy and happy.

CLOSURE AND MEANING

Viktor Frankl was a gifted Austrian psychiatrist who suffered the Holocaust of World War II at first hand. Imprisoned in Auschwitz and other concentration camps, he emerged from the war with an intense interest in helping people cope with the immense suffering they had gone through.

Viktor Frankl's book *Man's Search for Meaning*, Boston, Beacon Press, 1959, is an inspiring example of coping with suffering beyond the comprehension of most of us. Frankl has been very influential on current views about coping and unhappiness.

From thinking about his own experience and his tremendous powers of observation, Frankl noticed that prisoners who had a sense of purpose in their lives and who also saw meaning in their suffering were the ones who survived the longest and who coped the best. He even came to believe that these prisoners were subconsciously avoided by guards conducting 'random' selections of people for the gas chambers. Frankl recognised that when we find meaning in a situation, such as *'Surviving my suffering at the hands of the Nazis is important so I can bear witness to the world on behalf of all my friends and family'* it enables us to place the experience in context or to make some sense of it.

Frankl quotes the German philosopher Nietzsche who said: 'He who has a *why* to live can bear with almost any *how*.'

Frankl was able to endure the degradations, brutality and senselessness of the concentration camp by focusing on images and memories of loved family and friends. He, like many others who must cope with awful realities, practised a grim humour, took solace in religion and even celebrated occasional moments of captivating beauty that occurred in a sunset or the snowy silhouette of a tree.

Frankl also believed that people can *transcend* or rise above stressful experiences, allowing those experiences to pass and not live on in damaging ways in our thoughts and feelings. He described this by example: 'In the concentration camp every circumstance conspires to make the prisoner lose his hold. All the familiar goals in life are snatched away. What alone remains is… the ability to choose one's attitude in a given set of circumstances.'

Frankl is telling us that it is discovering what is truly meaningful to us, and behaving in ways that are in tune with those abiding values, that can provide a deep strength and ability to cope. One of the practical ways of doing this is to be very clear about what is important and vital in our lives, and to distinguish them from those events that will pass and are of lesser consequence. Later in this chapter you will find exercises to help you identify what is important to you.

HARDINESS

A different approach from Frankl was taken by American psychologist Suzanne Kobasa. Kobasa studied a large number of executives who operated in large and stressful organisations. As she predicted, many of these individuals suffered anxiety and disease, and performed less effectively in their jobs as a result.

Kobasa was, however, more intrigued by a smaller number of executives who experienced the same stresses and tough business environment as the others, but who did not get ill. After examining closely their attitudes and observing their behaviour, she outlined three factors that seemed to define the difference between the healthy executives and the sick ones. Lumping these factors together, she termed the difference *hardiness.*

Suzanne Kobasa, 'Stressful life events, personality and health: an enquiry into hardiness', *Journal of Personality and Social Psychology*, 1979 37(1), 1-11.

Firstly Kobasa found there was a strong link between the healthier executives and their feelings of being in *control*. They did not feel powerless in the face of external pressures and demands, but instead felt themselves to be in charge of whatever happened to them.

Second, the executives who stayed healthy in Kobasa's investigation demonstrated a *commitment* to things they judged important and meaningful. She found many different things that were meaningful; relationships and family, social institutions, church and politics, as well as work. The executives had a deep involvement in more than just one aspect of life, so their jobs didn't totally define them as people.

Kobasa and others suspect that what is meaningful may not in itself be important: what matters is that we act in concert with those things in our lives that we believe to be important.

The third aspect of hardiness is *flexibility*. It means viewing any new event or life change as a challenge. Kobasa's hardy executives responded with energy and creativity to what life threw at them, adapted to the situation and tried new approaches if old ones didn't work.

So Kobasa's hardy individuals seemed to be prepared to live life to the full, to be productive and competent, and to respond to life's challenges with energy and commitment. The key is that these people *felt* that they were in control and therefore viewed stresses as challenges.

A related idea is the notion of *optimism*. A study which looked at recovery from major heart surgery found that optimists – defined as people who have a consistent, general expectation that good things will happen – recovered better than others did, and reached recovery milestones (such as walking unaided) faster. Even when things go wrong, optimists seem to be able to shrug off their misfortunes and get on with their lives. One large American insurance company now uses a measure of optimism to select its sales staff in the belief that they can better handle the knocks and setbacks of selling life insurance.

See a controversial book by the father of this concept, Martin Seligman, called *What You Can Change and What you Can't*, Random House, 1994.

SENSE OF COHERENCE

While Kobasa was reporting her work with executives, a sociologist on the other side of the world published a theory that was remarkably consistent with the ideas of both Frankl and Kobasa. Aaron Antonovsky, an Israeli, spent many hours interviewing Jewish survivors of the Holocaust. He had predicted that these survivors would still be suffering many years after the events. He was right, and found many survivors suffered nightmares, depression and a number of stress-related medical conditions.

Aaron Antonovsky, *Health, Stress and Coping*, New York, Josey Bass, 1979

But Antonovsky was also fascinated by a number of people who showed no physical or emotional ill effects, who didn't have nightmares or any other symptoms, despite the horrors they had endured. Why had they coped so well? What are the factors that cause people to remain healthy under stress?

Again, there were three key points. All the healthy survivors saw their worlds as *manageable, meaningful and comprehensible.*

Not long before his death in 1994, Antonovsky spoke at the annual health psychology conference in New Zealand. He described his three concepts this way:

> **By comprehensible** *we mean that the world has a structure that I as a person understand. Comprehensible means that I know the rules, or that I know things work in this way for reasons that I understand, even if they are horrible, terrible things. In other words: 'Life ain't a fair game, but I know how to stay in it'.*
>
> **By manageable** *it means that I have the resources at my disposal to manage this situation. It means I have what it takes to handle this thing, whether that requires material resources or friends and acquaintances or my own self-esteem and brain!*

For Antonovsky, like Frankl, *meaningfulness* was the most important of these attributes. The others are important, but if nothing in your life has meaning; if you don't see a purpose and meaning in living, then you don't have the will or desire to manage any situation which arises.

A person who is confident that their world is comprehensible, manageable and invested with meaning is operating with a strong sense of *coherence*. Antonovsky believed that this sense of coherence is a key factor in good coping.

CHECK YOUR OWN EXPERIENCE

Have you noticed that there are times when you've coped better with problems than at others? What is it that made the difference? Can you think of individuals who seem to cope really well, no matter what life throws at them? Why do you think some people don't seem to get depressed or strung out or lose their cool?

Take a minute to list what you think are the secrets of people who cope well:

THE SECRETS OF PEOPLE WHO COPE WELL

_____
_____
_____
_____
_____
_____
_____

How did you do? Did any of your 'success secrets' appear in what science tells us? Our list would look like this:

THE SECRETS OF PEOPLE WHO COPE WELL

- *Believe that they have some control over what happens to them, and control only those things they can.*

- *Are involved in what is important to them and find meaning in things other than just a job (for example).*

- *Respond to anything life sends as a challenge, are energetic and resourceful in coping.*

- *Understand the rules for living: life makes sense even if it is not sensible.*

- *Know what to do to cope and how to get the resources needed.*

- *Know their reasons for living.*

How do we put these concepts into practice when faced with stress-inducing life crises? New Zealand psychologist Geoffrey Ruthe spent many years working with children who were dying from cancer and with their families. He often observed that as the children became more ill, the world of the parents narrowed and focused on the thing that truly was most important to them. For families whose children weren't going to recover, the initial hopes and concerns for long-term health and even a cure for the child were replaced with the need to have a pain-free day or to enjoy a birthday out of hospital. When faced with situations over which they had no control (the illness), the parents repeatedly switched their attention to achievable, smaller events they could realistically influence.

GETTING CLEAR ON VALUES

In our experience the most important step in effective coping is developing a clear understanding about what is important in our lives.

Have you ever seen a child crumple up in tears and distress because she didn't get the ice-cream she wanted? Do you remember how frustrated and angry you got because your parents wouldn't allow you to stay up later than you wanted and watch your favourite TV programme? As an adult, do you feel upset or cheated somehow because you are unable to have the dishwasher your neighbours have, or the car of your dreams, or a holiday trip to the islands?

Human beings are infused with a complicated set of rules for determining when they are happy. Being thwarted in our 'wants' is a sure-fire recipe for being distressed and unhappy. The gap between what we want and what we have is one of the greatest contributors to stress. And ironically, it is all caused by our perceptions and beliefs about what is important.

Many times in our practice we have been confronted with people who are working very hard, but who complain of feeling unfulfilled or of never 'making it'. When pushed to be more specific, it is curious to find that 'making it' is very hard for them to define. 'How will you know when you're "made"?' we ask.

The umms and ahhhs that this question produces are remarkable. In fact the question seems to upset some people quite a lot. "What do you mean, how will I know?". "What a thing to ask? How *can* you know – it's just important to keep on working", they say. (You can change the word 'working' for almost anything – 'providing for the family', 'paying the mortgage', 'sucking up to my clients').

Take the example of Nick, a young man of about 30 who had recently married. His new wife came from a family which greatly prided itself on its material success and standing in the community. Nick was an exceptionally stable type. He led a busy but satisfying life; he worked, he went fishing a great deal, he hung out with his friends and he steadily worked away at renovating his small house. After he had been married for about 18 months, he was referred to us by his doctor. He described feeling unhappy and dissatisfied, but he was surprised by this, because his wife was about to have a baby and he was overjoyed at the prospect of being a father.

When we reviewed what had been happening in his life recently, Nick spent quite a lot of time describing how nice his new family was, and how kind his wife's brothers and sisters had been toward them. Since being in the family, he had been inundated with advice and offers of help to renovate his house. One brother-in-law had spent a lot of time talking with Nick about how to maximise the potential return on his home, and where he could move to when he sold it. Another had told Nick that he should accumulate information from his work (in a government department) and then set himself up as a consultant. Nick had listened and been impressed with the advice. At work, he had started to do courses on quality management techniques to advance himself.

Nick was surprised when he realised how much time he spent talking with us about his wife's family. He began to see that they had an unwritten set of rules about how to be happy and successful which they were passing on to him. Without being conscious of it, Nick had begun to measure himself by these rules.

After a few more sessions (which involved Nick's wife and the newborn baby) Nick made a decision to go back to his own rules. After all, he reasoned, he had a job that enabled him to be home by 4.30 every day to see his new baby, was enjoyable without being stressful, paid well enough for him to have the mortgage paid off in

15 years, and had a superannuation scheme that would let him retire at 50. As his wife said, 'Life could be a whole lot worse than this!'

Nick provided a very good example of the sort of stress that can occur when people live their lives according to what someone else tells them is good for them. People who every day act in ways that are out of tune with their values end up feeling compromised, cheated or manipulated.

The famous psychoanalyst Eric Fromm spent a long time trying to understand how it was that people in his adopted country, America, whose lives were so much better than those of people in Europe, were so unhappy. He decided that it was because, in America, people spent their lives trying to:

- *Have* enough (money, resources, 'things'), so that they can:
- *Do* what they want (in terms of work, how they spend their time), because then they can:
- *Be* happy.

Unfortunately, most people get stuck at the first step. They never 'have' enough.

Perhaps you've said to yourself, 'When I have the house paid off I'm going to make a change, slow down, do what I want'. Then when the house was paid off, you said, 'After I buy a new car, then I'm going to make a change'. One day you reach the end of your life and realise you've never done all the things you really wanted to.

Fromm wrote many books that are worth reading. The one in which he talked about these ideas is called *To Have or To Be*, Harper and Row, New York 1976.

Fromm said that to have a satisfying life you need to invert the formula. First, you need to:

- *Be* who you are. Know your strengths, weaknesses, your purpose. This self-awareness will lead you to:
- *Do* what you love. This doing will be the contribution of your unique gifts. Because you are giving yourself away, you will be rewarded, and:
- *Have* what you need. Life provides no guarantees that you will have everything you want!

As a well-known proverb has it: *There are two ways to be rich: one is to have more, the other is to want less.*

How do you turn the *having/doing/being* cycle around?

- You stop making having money the goal.
- You stop being driven by shoulds ('I should have a good car/job/house').
- You stop measuring success by your bank account and possessions.
- You get your priorities in order and follow your heart, guided by your values.

The being mode of living means that you are going to be more connected to what is really important to you.

Archangel adapted from Iain McCormack book, "Coping with Change"

Archangel Activity

This exercise helps you think about what is truly important in your life.

Imagine that you are travelling somewhere in a car and suddenly time stops. A beautiful angel appears before you and says:

'I am sent to give you a choice. In less than one second you'd have been involved in a terrible disaster, but instead of accepting what will happen, you may *choose* instead something you will lose and it will be lost forever! I have a list already prepared, and you must rank in order the items from 1 (most valued by you) through to 13 (least important to you). You've only got 10 minutes, because it's really hard to stop time, could you hurry it up?'

	Your sight through an accident
	Your hearing through an accident
	Your family through an accident
	Your mobility through loss of your legs
	Your closest friends other than your family
	Your freedom through being imprisoned for 10 years
	Your sense of purpose in life for ever
	Your current job
	Your savings
	Your home or place of dwelling
	Your reputation in the eyes of the public
	Your self-confidence and self-esteem
	All your personal belongings through a burglary

Think carefully about this exercise. Write down your answers to the following questions:

What reasons did you have for your two highest valued choices?

Number 1

_____
_____
_____
_____

Number 2

_____
_____
_____
_____

How does the importance of each value impact on your daily life – for example, how much time do you allocate to your two highest valued choices?

_____
_____
_____
_____

Would someone who observed you be able to tell what is most important to you from how you spend your everyday life?

_____

_____

_____

_____

This exercise seems to prompt people to wonder whether they are *truly* behaving in accord with their values, that their lives are operating with the right priorities. The important question, of course, is whether *you* believe your life represents the things that you value. We suggest that you do this exercise with your partner or family and ask them to comment on whether what you *say* you value is reflected in how you act.

The Power of Believing You Have Control

Many researchers have investigated the link between the amount of control people feel in their lives and a variety of consequences. In an experiment typical of the approach, researchers examined how well a large group of people could perform a boring addition task under conditions of very loud noise. The twist in the experiment was that half the group were told that they just had to cope as best they could with the noise, while the other half were told that they could turn off the noise if they had to, but please to try just to cope. The experimenters examined the results and found that on average the people who could ask to turn off the noise added up their columns of numbers faster and more accurately than the no-control group. Dramatically, however, no one asked to turn the sound off! It was the knowledge they had control that appeared to make the difference.

CHAPTER 6

Changing your thinking

Have you ever been in the situation of waiting for a family member or lover to arrive and he or she is late? As time goes by you will probably notice the quality of your thoughts change, starting out with reassuring, rational explanations for the lapse and ending up with scenes of mayhem, disaster and car crashes: 'This isn't normal, she's usually on time and reliable. It's a bit out of character. What could have happened? Bloody annoying. Now we'll be late. I feel stupid standing here. People will think I've been stood up. Hope she's OK. Not a crash or anything? Hell, now I'm worried. How could I find out?... '

Or do you get on with what you are doing, wondering occasionally what happened to delay them, but saying things to yourself like, 'Well there's no point worrying, because that won't change anything'?

It is a sure-fire bet that if your thoughts lead you down the 'catastrophe' path, you will trigger the stress response and suffer growing feelings of anxiety, nervousness and upset. As we saw in chapter 4, there is a kind of self-reinforcing loop that exists between thinking and stress, and that operates at a physiological level in our brains. Anxious thoughts can trigger the physical stress response in our bodies, which in turn leads us to think at a lower, more reactive, emotive level.

Ironically, because of all that arousal (remember that the stress response is a call to action), it is quite likely that when the person you waited for does arrive, you will discharge the tension *that you created* by telling them off and getting angry. The stress you caused yourself in that situation has been generated entirely from the images and thoughts you used to explain the delay in their arrival.

But is it possible to change thoughts, especially when sometimes we are not even aware they are there? Some scientists believe that there are differing levels to our thinking: that while we are aware of some thoughts, others occur too quickly for us to register them, or occur so often that we become 'blind' to them. This type of thinking is called 'unconscious' or 'automatic'. It is this automatic thinking that we are interested in, because it is through this that much unnecessary stress arises.

The diagram below describes how thoughts become automatic, similar to the process of forming a habit.

As an example, take driving. As children there was a time when we didn't know that we couldn't drive. Lacking the skills and the awareness of those skills is called *unconscious incompetence* (Stage 1 below).

Levels of Thinking

	Aware of thoughts	
3 Conscious competence *I can do it, but I have to think about it*		**Conscious incompetence 2** *I know that I can't do it!*
Unconscious competence *I can do it without 4 thinking about it!*	Blind to thoughts	**Unconscious incompetence** *I don't know that I don't know* 1

Then, after watching Mum and Dad drive, and pretending to drive ourselves, awareness dawns and we realise that we want to drive, but can't – the skill simply isn't there. This is called *conscious incompetence* (Stage 2).

Then, after years of cajoling and waiting for the legal age to arrive, Mum and Dad finally agree to lessons! In the first few lessons the mysterious skills associated with clutches, handbrakes and tachometers are performed poorly and in a self-conscious way. Mentally we rehearse our actions and talk ourselves through the steps to do, correcting and commenting to ourselves on how we are going. This is the stage called *conscious competence* (Stage 3).

Eventually, with practice and time, our driving becomes more natural and unthinking and we 'automatically' perform the tasks we have to, without *conscious* thought. All the thinking and processing and talking we once did is unnecessary and has moved out of conscious awareness. This is the automatic stage called *unconscious competence* (Stage 4).

The implications for stress lie in the words 'automatic' and 'unconscious'. Through constant repetition we become skilled at viewing ourselves and the world in certain ways. Habits of thought and destructive ways of talking to ourselves become ingrained, 'natural' and unquestioned (or unconscious).

UNCONSCIOUS THOUGHTS

Unconscious thought is a key phrase. Just because we are unaware of our thoughts does not mean that they do not occur. The processing simply moves to a lower level. How many times have you driven a stretch of road whilst thinking about something other than the drive, only to get to your destination without recollection of the traffic conditions or journey?

It is exactly the same with emotions and stress. The limbic system can become used to responding in stressed ways if the quality of our experience is habitually tense, viewed as threatening or anxiety-provoking. Our thoughts play a large role in conditioning our stress response to remain inappropriately aroused. Even worse than that, we get used to feeling and thinking in these ways, regard them as 'normal' and never question whether our quality of life could be different.

Strong evidence exists to suggest that people do develop deeply ingrained habits of thought. Depressed individuals, for example, are shown to think more negative thoughts, and to have a tendency to view the world, themselves and the future much more pessimistically than non-depressed people. Likewise the thoughts of Type A personalities have been shown to contain consistent distortions or mistakes in their internal logic. Type A's show excessive concern with lateness or deadlines, and construct rather overdramatic scenarios about the consequences of being late. They often maintain hostile mental monologues about how hopeless this or that person is – but suppress the negative feelings that accompany the thoughts by bottling their emotions up and not showing them. No wonder they are candidates for heart disease!

Have a look at James Pennebaker's ideas for using disclosure as a stress management tool later in this book.

American psychology professor James Pennebaker has studied the effects of stress on health for some time and is convinced that one of the major factors affecting our response to stress is how we deal with negative emotions. Inhibiting negative emotions leads to ill-health, he believes. He quotes a fascinating story to illustrate what he means:

> *A 45-year-old bank vice-president was a suspect in an embezzlement investigation. When he was given a lie detection test his stress levels were very high as measured by his heart rate, blood pressure and skin conductance. This is normal for both innocent and guilty people. However his reactions went even higher when asked about the embezzlement, and with repeated questioning he broke down and confessed. The remarkable thing was that after confessing he let go completely and his physiological readings became very relaxed. Even though he was assured of going to jail, and his personal, professional and financial lives were ruined, he was more relaxed and assured of himself. When escorted out of the office he shook the hand of the man who conducted the lie detection test and thanked him for all he had done!*

Thoughts That Hurt

Imagine if we could plug a microphone into someone's head and hear their thoughts. Would we pick up a link between stress and what they say to themselves?

Aaron Beck, a noted American psychiatrist, described the case of a successful novelist who remained unhappy and pessimistic about his work despite financial rewards and public acclaim. On hearing a compliment about his work he became upset: 'People won't be honest with me. They *know* I'm mediocre. They just won't accept me as I really am. They keep giving me phoney compliments.'

A.T.Beck, *Cognitive Therapy and the Emotional Disorders*, New York, International Universities Press, 1976. Beck is highly regarded for his work in highlighting the impact of thinking on depressed mood states.

The source of this man's troubles lay not with his public, but with the way his own beliefs got in the way of his world view. All the compliments he heard were filtered and coloured by his own frame of reference, which was made up of doubts concerning his own ability and worth.

A well-known Australian cricketer discovered for himself how troubling self-talk can be. At the height of his career he experienced an unexplained loss of form. He had the attentions of many coaches and advisers, none of whom made any difference, and his form continued to plummet until his place in the national team was under threat. It seemed that the more he worried about it, the worse things got. He responded by trying even harder – a classic stress response – only to find that he wasn't getting the simple basics right, was making easy errors and fluffing skills he was known to be expert in. When things got to the point that he was vomiting before competition and shaking before play, he sought help from a sports psychologist.

With the help of the psychologist he examined the mental 'conversations' that he was having with himself, and saw that at least some of the trouble lay with the manner of his thinking. Here's an excerpt from the journal of thoughts he kept:

> '*Come on man, you've got to concentrate.*'
> '*I don't want this.*'
> '*I'm in trouble.*'
> '*They'll pick up that you're nervous and exploit it.*'
> '*Christ you're hopeless - you're just being lazy.*'

'Look at how you ballsed that up!'
'Oh, this is too much - I should retire now.'
'I'm a dead duck.'

Embedded in these mental phrases were some obvious *limiting beliefs* about himself. The cricketer was increasing his mental distress by accentuating his errors and building up expectations of failure. This in turn represented a major threat to his esteem and livelihood. The stress response was triggered inappropriately, producing high levels of tension and adrenaline, which had the effect of hampering his performance. The pessimistic thoughts left him feeling helpless and hopeless. This kind of thinking encourages people to give up before they start. In situations like this the pressure we feel from inside our own heads has more to do with how we end up feeling and behaving than with what actually happens.

Many people use this human tendency to be affected by limiting mental images and thoughts. In many sporting situations the opposition will deliberately play on any perceived weakness to 'psych out' their opponents. Barracking in softball and sledging in cricket are obvious examples. In boxing, Muhammed Ali was a master at this, telling his opponents 'You won't last the distance, you won't last the distance'. (We won't even talk about what happens in the political arena.)

Check the Yerkes-Dodson Law described in chapter 2, which explains this effect more fully.

But it works in a positive direction as well. Students in schools are being taught to visualise being calm during exams. Sportspeople are encouraged to visualise and think about winning images. Try experimenting with an image of you relaxing in a favourite spot next time you feel stressed.

LIMITING BELIEFS SPELT OUT

Here are some examples of limiting beliefs:

*I should do this better.
I can't cope.
This is just a disaster!
They don't care.
I just can't learn this.
People will think me stupid.
The company won't change.*

When people think negatively, they tend to act in ways that will not get them what they want. This creates a self-fulfilling prophesy: what you think is what you get.

Our colleague and friend Dr Iain McCormick has categorised the kinds of thinking that commonly lead to stress. He describes *Dangerous Drivers, Stupid Stoppers* and *Cunning Confusers.* Read through these with the aim of identifying those that sound like you.

Iain wrote a very helpful book called *Coping with Change,* Wellington, GP Books, 1988. We have used Iain's terms throughout this section.

Dangerous Drivers

From time to time it is helpful to tell ourselves to buck up or get on with the job. It certainly isn't harmful to seek improved performance or greater effort. But if we habitually goad ourselves into straining beyond our limits or striving for too long a time, the result will be feelings of pressure and strain.

Many people who are Type A personalities come equipped with a fully operational set of dangerous drivers:

- BE PERFECT

   This driver operates in a way that says we should *never* make a mistake. If we do it will be a disaster, intolerable. We are not allowed to make mistakes, and we should be upset if anyone else does. In fact, it's better to do all the work ourselves, because only then we can be sure.

- HURRY UP

   This is a trap that seems to get worse under stress. People in this trap get terribly upset if a delay occurs. Waiting for someone is agony. Lateness in ourselves and others produces complaints and irritation (verbal and/or mental). We can spot the trap in demands to be hasty in our work or through rushing others along.

- BE STRONG

  This driver operates to stop people showing their feelings or admitting to some weakness or need ('It would be weak', 'They'd think I'm not coping'). We maintain pressure on ourselves to keep going.

- NEVER SAY NO

  There seems to be an inbuilt tendency for many people to feel bad if they turn down someone's request, or if they refuse an offer. Many sales techniques are structured around this piece of psychology. The stress results from ending up with too much on, conflicting commitments or no space for our own needs.

To discover dangerous drivers in your thoughts, look for words like *should, ought, must, can't*. The test for determining whether a dangerous driver is unhealthy in your life is if you are feeling pressured or harried when others seem to be coping.

Stupid Stoppers

Thoughts that prevent us from doing certain activities or interrupt our performance are 'stupid stoppers'. Stupid stoppers lead to anxiety or fear, and begin a chain of irrational thoughts that artificially impose limits on our actions or wants.

- CATASTROPHISING

  One of the most poignant areas in which to observe catastrophising is in adolescent life. Teenagers get terribly upset and irritable as they wade through complexities of what is cool and what isn't, the rigours of love and liking, and the importance of fitting in. Remember feeling that your life would end because your mother collected you from the cinema? Or that your friends gave you a hard time because your parents wouldn't let you wear your hair in a particular style? That's catastrophising, believing it would be awful, terrible, a disaster, a nightmare, a terminal embarrassment if something occurred.

The Cost of Catastrophising

As a teenager I was terribly keen on a girl at my school. I really wanted to ask her out, but was worried she'd say no. First I tried to tell her I loved her in all the usual ways – I tripped her up, stood on her sandal and constantly borrowed her pens. Nothing magical happened except that she hit me (I treasured the bruise for days). So then I asked all her friends, 'If I asked her out (not that I want to), would she say yes?'. They all laughed and said 'probably'. I conferred with all my mates, who urged me to give it a go. One night I stood by the telephone and dialled her number. I hung up. I dialled again. I hung up. Ten times I did this! Visions of her saying 'no' swam before me. I pictured myself having to walk around at school with 'loser' tattooed on my forehead. I knew that the knowledge of her saying no would be telepathically transferred to all my friends, who would laugh and despise me. I didn't call.

Years later, I was in a shop and saw my unrequited love. We got chatting and went for a coffee. I confessed to her that years ago I had been desperately in love with her. She laughed and said, 'Well why didn't you ask me out? I always hoped you would.'

- JUDGING COMMENTARY

    If we think back to our athlete, or to Beck's writer, we can see how self-criticism can lead to high levels of stress and unhappiness. It is certainly not an exaggeration to say that constant self-criticism can lead people to take their own lives. The negative self-labelling that we engage in helps shape our views about what is and isn't possible for us. We engage in such thinking at our peril. Remember that much of this type of thinking may be habitual and automatic – we may not know that we are doing it.

Stupid stoppers are able to be detected when we notice that we are highly anxious, frightened or unduly worried by an event. Look for *'if – then'* statements, or *disaster scenarios* or *negative self-labels and put-downs*.

Cunning Confusers

These are the ways in which we engage in psychological trickery to distort reality and get us off the hook as far as *personal responsibility* is concerned. This trap causes stress by avoiding our feelings, or by allowing us not to face up to the truth about a situation.

- BLAMING

    Blaming works when we say things like, 'You make me unhappy', or 'Working with Sarah drives me crazy.' Do these things really have such an impact? Do other people or circumstances cause us to feel these things? Our feelings are not passed on to us by someone else.

    Reactions are not handed out at the start of every situation we get involved in. How we feel depends on how we view a situation and what we *say in our minds*. Directing blame at another will cause us stress, because we will have shelved any responsibility for fixing the situation – the ball is now in their court. How often does it happen that we get frustrated or stressed out because another person hasn't done what we *wanted* them to do?

- EXAGGERATION

    This trap is similar to catastrophising. Many times people will become upset because they exaggerate the importance of a particular circumstance in their lives. Weight is a good example of how this trap can cause stress: have you observed a friend become upset because they see themselves as fat, when they don't look like it to you? This trap leads people to set up win–lose scenarios, such as 'If only I could have a Porsche, then my life would be perfect.'

To judge whether you have fallen into this trap of cunning confusers, look for *flawed logic* and no possibility of argument. *All-or-nothing* statements ('I *never* get a night out') or 'just because' arguments are also a good sign of these traps.

Limiting Beliefs Exercise

Try to identify the limiting beliefs that appear in the following case:

Geoffrey works as a junior researcher in a medium-sized firm. He has an important presentation to senior management coming up and doesn't want it to go badly. He worries that he cannot speak well and that he will forget what to say. He is sure that if this happens it will be the end of his career, and people will mark him as a loser. The fact that Shirley (the accountant) will be at the presentation makes it worse. Twice she's said how much she's looking forward to the meeting, and from the smile she's given him he can tell she doesn't like him.

Glancing at the clock Geoffrey experiences a feeling of panic: only six hours to go! As he feels his heart pound, he wonders if he will make it – he hates himself for getting so worked up, but he also hates disappointing people. He starts to go over his notes for the fourth time...

What are the limiting beliefs operating here?

Write down what we would point out to Geoffrey to convince him that his thinking is negatively affecting his feelings (and undoubtedly his performance):

_____
_____
_____
_____
_____
_____
_____

WHICH TRAPS?

Developing a good understanding of which traps are sabotaging your thinking is vital to changing them. Familiarity with the traps described above will enable us to recognise them as they occur, allowing us to 'catch ourselves' in time to change. We can then engage in some argument or positive discussion with ourselves to adapt our thinking to a positive, less stressful style.

It may feel a bit strange when we first begin to try to challenge and change our thinking – we might feel self-conscious and hesitant. In order to break a thought habit, the first step is to make it very obvious when we do it and that may mean we go back to the stage of feeling awkward and uncomfortable. *That is a good sign.* It means that we have moved from the 'unconscious box' to one of the 'conscious boxes' described at the start of this chapter.

The Diary Method of Capturing Thoughts

Since we want to look out for patterns and habits of thought, we have designed a *thought diary* in which we record the situations and thoughts which cause us to feel stressed. You may like to copy the format into a small notebook to carry with you.

There are 5 columns to complete in the diary.

Date and time: Do you get stressed at certain times, or on certain days?

Situation: Describe the situation in detail. What happened? Who was there? Are there recurring circumstances that cause you stress? These may be both external and internal circumstances.

Thoughts: Write your thoughts down verbatim. Do not judge or censor your thoughts – just write down what you become aware of. (You are also allowed to swear in your thoughts.)

Rating: Measure your stress in each situation by rating out of 10. 1 equates to quite calm and relaxed, 5 equates to moderate stress, 10 equates to mad panic!

Trap: Identify which trap your thinking has fallen into. Do you tend to repeat the same thinking mistakes?

Using the example of Geoffrey above, we have filled out some of the entries.

Date/time	Describe the situation in detail	My thoughts	1-10	Which trap?
Mon. am.	Met Shirley in hall - she smiled	She's just trying to be nice - I know she hates me	7	Blame
Mon. am.	Rehearsing notes - felt terrible	I know this will be a disaster. I have to get this right or else I'll lose my job! I know I can't do it	9	Catastrophising Be perfect Catastrophising again! Be perfect
Mon. pm.	Preparing for meeting - felt rushed and sick	No time left! I can't look bad	10+	Hurry up Catastrophising again! Be strong

Becoming Aware of Your Thoughts

There are three steps to this process:

1. **Becoming aware of your thoughts**

    Although very simple, this method has proved its worth time and again. Use the diary for two solid weeks. You will find the first few times awkward, but it will soon become easier.

2. **Discovering which traps cause you stress**

    It is vital to identify the limiting beliefs which are sabotaging your thinking.

3. **Disputing your negative self-talk**

    The most important step in this process is to challenge your thinking, and to replace negative thoughts with more positive, realistic and calming statements. At the start of this process this will also seem strange. It is important to persevere. Remember it has taken you all the years of your life to think in a stressed way – give yourself a few months to change and think differently!

Talk to Yourself

To change from negative and destructive thinking to a more healthy style, it is important to begin to *challenge* your thinking. It isn't cast in stone. It is quite healthy and normal for people to evaluate their thoughts and responses, so try not to feel self-conscious when you talk to yourself. As Margit Brew describes:

> *I have trimmed my language of 'shoulds' and 'musts' and 'ought tos' and 'have tos'. It has freed me more for activities where I can express my creative potential. I have also pruned most – almost all – 'onlys' and 'justs'... I will not limit my world in that way. The body in its language of wellness or illness shows us how well we approach life. To this end I have abolished every 'can't' in my life as 'can'ts' have a paralysing effect.*

Margit describes a thought*ful* approach to mental life. She does not act as the passive recipient of her own thoughts, but is prepared to challenge and train herself to consider things differently. This epitomises the approach we advocate.

Let's return to the example of Geoffrey and see how we might 'cleanup' his thinking and have him develop a more thoughtful style:

Date/ time	Describe the situation in detail	My thoughts	Re-framed thoughts
Mon. am.	Met Shirley in hall - she smiled	She's just trying to be nice - I know she hates me	Maybe she genuinely likes me - no one else thinks she's mean.
Mon. am.	Rehearsing notes - felt terrible	I know this will be a disaster. I have to get this right or else I'll lose my job! I know I can't do it	I've done good work. I don't know of anyone who lost a job over a muffed presentation. They must think I'm OK if I was asked to do the presentation!
Mon. pm.	Preparing for meeting - felt rushed and sick	No time left! I can't look bad	I need to calm down - try some deep breaths. I'll survive this.

The thoughts in the right-hand column represent a much more considered, rational style. Compare them to the comments you made earlier about Geoffrey's case. It is quite likely that you wrote similar things *because you were dispassionate.* Bringing our thinking back to a rational, less emotionally dominated level is a key to effective stress management.

We have developed some specific messages that will help you to challenge those thinking traps:

Disputing Dangerous Drivers
BE PERFECT:
Ask 'Who says?', or 'What will really happen?' or 'What's the worst thing that will occur if I make an error?'

e.g. Instead of, 'Oh no, what a fool I am, I must not miss my appointment', try:

'Who says I'm not allowed to forget the occasional appointment?'

HURRY UP:
Ask *'What is the reasonable time that is required?'*, or remind yourself to 'under-promise, over-deliver', or simply slow down. It's better to arrive late than to die trying.

BE STRONG:
Ask *'Would I allow other people to feel hurt/angry/sad in this situation?'* or *'Who says I have to be strong?'*

e.g. Instead of 'I can't let them see how they upset me', try seizing the bull by the horns and courageously saying:

'When you ignored my report I felt angry. I want to go back and examine the issues it raised.'

NEVER SAY NO:
Remind yourself of your limits and coping abilities. Remember that people generally feel better knowing where others stand. Don't commit to things you don't want to.

e.g. Instead of 'Aw Mum, I don't want…oh all right then, I'll fit it in today', try:

'I can do it, Mum, but I'd prefer to wait until tomorrow.'

Disputing Stupid Stoppers
CATASTROPHISING:
Saying *'So what if…'* is a good way of diluting the effect of a faith in disasters. Try *'Will that really happen?'*, or deliberately run through to the end of all possible disasters by saying, *'What would happen then? And if that occurred what would happen then?'*

e.g. Instead of 'If I ask him out and he says "no" it would be too embarrassing for me to bear', try:

'I'll be sad if he says no, but the sun will still rise tomorrow, and nothing ventured, nothing gained.'

Or try:

'If he says "no" I'll be stuck at home again, and never meet another man and grow old watching "Coronation Street", which I hate, and then my friends would be asking me what happened and come round to have "Coronation Street" parties – and hey , I might just do that instead.'

Disputing Cunning Confusers

By their nature, these are the hardest to change. Often cunning confusers will exist in a cloud of their own logic. To change out of this trap requires a great commitment to *take responsibility* for your own actions and to find out what the *reality* is, rather than relying on your prejudices or beliefs.

To do this, gather information, ask questions and seek facts. Take responsibility for your own feelings and your own actions. Try not to blame other people for how you feel. Be in charge of your own life as much as you can be.

e.g. Instead of 'I'm really hassled by the boss. He has come down on me twice today – he's just a jerk. Maybe I'm better off on the dole', try:

'I'm really hassled by the boss. He has come down on me twice today – I'd better confront him and find out what's going on.'

Develop a Positive Belief Set

If you are interested, try a sample of Ellis' work in his book *Growth Through Reason: Verbatim Cases in Rational Emotive Psychotherapy*, Palo Alto, Behavioural Science Books, 1971. He's a very entertaining read.

Albert Ellis, a bombastic and challenging person whom Kay encountered on a number of his workshops, strongly believes that people are responsible for the misery and stress they feel because they stupidly accept what occurs in their heads as reality, and live by very strict rules. His message to people is to lighten up! Give yourself permission to make the occasional mistake. Don't dwell on it as if it were a disaster. You're human, aren't you? Well, humans *all* make mistakes. You are very unlikely to go through life without the occasional bad day, or fight, or late appointment, or nasty boss. Acknowledge that you will be disappointed by others; that life won't always go the way you want.

Ellis reportedly loved the Rolling Stones singing one particular song: *'You can't always get what you want – but if you try sometimes, you just might get what you need'.*

THE IMPORTANCE OF HUMOUR

Norman Cousins, an American journalist, developed a degenerative disease that his doctors told him stood very little chance of cure. Cousins, however, refused to believe that his situation was hopeless and spent his days watching funny films and re-runs of *Candid Camera*. The show's host, Alan Funt, was an acquaintance of Cousins and he supplied him with other material and out-takes from the series that never made it to air. Cousins spent his days chuckling and laughing, and reading humourous stories. Amazingly, he recovered. Cousins' case is not isolated, but it attracted much attention as he was well known and the case well documented.

Norman Cousins, *Anatomy of an Illness as Perceived by a Patient: Reflections on Healing and Regeneration*, New York, W.W. Norton, 1979.

Hutt Hospital in New Zealand, runs clinics in which patients are taken to see comedians and funny films as part of their recovery. Serious research into humour (pardon our oxymoron) suggests recovery times are faster for people who are encouraged to laugh.

Speculation about the healing effects of laughter centre around the physical movement of muscles and the relaxation of the diaphragm. Other studies have suggested that the immune response is actually boosted by laughing, and that the release of catecholamines and endorphins that occurs when we laugh suppresses our response to pain.

Humour has a great effect in helping establish some distance and perspective. Finding the funny side in a situation changes your view of it. Although probably an urban myth, a great story is told about a man standing in court awaiting sentence for a small driving infringement. 'Well,' said the judge sternly, 'have you anything to say for yourself?' Casting his eyes heavenward, the man exclaimed loudly, 'Beam me up, Scotty!'

Humour can also dramatically defuse the tension in situations. In the middle of a tense standoff between anti-apartheid demonstrators and the police during the 1981 Springbok rugby tour of New Zealand, while both groups stood eye to eye, with the police behind their riot shields nervously fingering their batons, and the protesters chanting loudly and pushing and swaying forward, one man began to whistle the theme from the old police show *Z-Cars*. Surprisingly, both police and protesters began to giggle and then laugh. The crowd eventually moved off and violence was averted.

Here's a sign we saw on the back of a car once: *Eat a small toad every morning: it will be the worst thing you do all day.*

Laughing often and looking for the funny side of a situation dramatically changes our view of it. Spending time with people who make us laugh, and telling funny anecdotes and stories leads to a greater sense of enjoyment of life.

POSITIVE BELIEFS AND MENTAL REHEARSAL

One last point on thoughts and stress. Imagine how we would feel if all day we had to listen to a Walkman that played nothing but negative messages and constant self-criticism? When we ask people to listen in to their thoughts (by using the diary technique) they are often amazed at how much negative talk and self-criticism they engage in.

Try playing a different tape. Here are some ideas for a more positive belief system:

- At the end of each day reflect on at least three good things you did, and spend time basking in the achievement.

- Keep a 'brag file' of positive evaluations, compliments and nice comments. Take it out when you feel bad and remember each one. Take it out when you feel good, and smile!

- Enjoy the environment around you. Drink in the sights; absorb the sounds and tastes of wherever you are. Indulge your senses.

- Spend time in positive mental rehearsal. Instead of visualising what will go wrong, spend time picturing a successful outcome. Once a radical idea, this is now standard practice in athletics.

- Set challenging goals that will stimulate you. Surprise yourself with a realistic challenge.
- Celebrate your successes. Take time to recognise and reward yourself for achieving.
- Develop an attitude of gratitude. Count your blessings – life could be worse!

In the space below, write limiting beliefs you have become aware of and rewrite them as positive, empowering beliefs.

Limiting belief:

_____

_____

Empowering belief:

_____

_____

Limiting belief:

_____

_____

Empowering belief:

_____

_____

CHAPTER 7

Physical relaxation

Signs of tension can also be produced merely from our thinking. Anxious, worrying or angry thoughts can turn on the stress response equally as well as a physical situation, leading to tension and physical arousal. Remember, for example, that in the days before fathers attended births they had to wait outside the delivery room. The old stereotype of the 'expectant father' had him pacing nervously back and forth. The pacing occurred because the tremendous physical urge to *do something* could not be directed into useful action. Similarly, if you have ever had to wait while in a state of nervousness or excitement, you will realise how difficult it is to keep still.

Try an experiment. Ask another person to recall an incident that made them really angry or upset, and that hasn't yet been resolved. Get them to describe it and remember it as clearly and deeply as they can. Have them describe how it made them feel, what they wanted to do.

While your subject is describing and remembering what annoyed them, closely observe what happens to the talker's face, jaw, neck, shoulders, arms and hands. Did you observe any of the signs below?

After 5 minutes, stop and share what you saw. Allow the talker to come back down, and remind them that this is just an exercise.

PHYSICAL SIGNS OF TENSION

Faster breathing (especially from the chest)

Perspiration

Shoulders held high

Clenched jaw

Hands in fists, white knuckles

Frowns even in repose

Shaking, tremor

Abnormal clumsiness

Back pain

Frequent changes of posture or position

Darting eyes

Soreness of muscles

Closed posture, tightly folded arms

Stiffness in neck

Jerky movement or gait

If you read chapters 2, 3 and 4, you will have learnt about the effects on the body of stress. One of the most common reactions that stress produces is an increase in what is called *muscle tonus,* or what we recognise as tension. The type of tension that occurs during stress is designed to prepare us to act in some way, and if we observe people under stress they often appear tense, fidgety or overactive.

In fact, we often have to apply some willpower to *stop* ourselves from moving. Ironically this can also produce tension as we tighten our muscles to maintain control. Have you ever woken at night, convinced you heard the sounds of a burglar? The effort required to stay still when you are frightened but dare not move for fear of making a sound or to hear what is going on can be physically very tiring and draining.

People under chronic stress seem to take this tension so much for granted that they assume it is 'normal' to be uptight and tense. Sometimes this occurs without our thinking about it. We might be surprised by someone telling us we're frowning or scowling, or saying we look 'uptight'.

This occurs because our muscles are constantly adjusting themselves to what we do, whether it is drinking a cup of tea, walking along a road or wrestling with a knotty problem. A sense called *proprioception* enables us unconsciously to monitor our internal state and make many tiny internal adjustments to our physical state, so that, for example, we can keep our balance. Much of the time we do not *think* about keeping our balance – our brain and body happily co-ordinate in the background to keep us level. Because this process of adjustment is unconscious, and because we tend not to heed the messages from our bodies (at least consciously), we can become habituated to high levels of tension and stress. In effect, we learn not to notice signs of tension and stress.

This idea is linked to our earlier discussion about unconscious competence on page 69.

RELAXATION

The opposite of tension is relaxation. Relaxation is not blobbing out in front of the TV, or knocking back a few cans of lager. The type of relaxation discussed in this chapter occurs through a more active 'letting go' of tension. Relaxation produces a quiet body and a calm mind. Check the physical signs of relaxation in the table opposite. Relaxing our muscles sends the brain a message that all is well, and it is an effective way of lowering the arousal that accompanies stress. It produces an effect in the body which is the reverse of the stress reaction.

The rest of this chapter explains how you can achieve a relaxed and calm body. This skill is essential first aid in reducing your stress levels. Try these exercises out and continue with the ones that suit you best. *The important thing is to keep on using them.*

Read about the way the stress response is inhibited via the parasympathetic nervous system on page 51.

PHYSICAL SIGNS OF RELAXATION

Heart rate slows
Breathing rate slows
Breathing from abdomen
Longer breaths
Muscles loosen and unwind
Forehead smooth
Swallowing less often
Shoulders drop
Body becomes still and quiet
Eyelids droop or close
Lips part slightly, jaw relaxes
Reduced sweating

Relaxation exercises discussed in this section offer a methodical way to physiologically change the body to a calm, less aroused state. This will positively affect both the body and the mind. Studies investigating a variety of relaxation strategies demonstrate that people who regularly indulge in relaxation tend to be less reactive, less fatigued and less anxious. They report improved sleep, fewer worries and an improved sense of well-being. Regularly using techniques for relaxing can lower our overall levels of tension and cushion us against overstress.

If we watch sportspeople on television we may see them perform very similar exercises at particularly pressured or crucial times. It is very common for athletes to modify their state of physical and psychological arousal in accordance with the Yerkes-Dodson Law that we met in chapter 2.

If we use relaxation techniques when in a stressful situation, we can remain calm, move away from distressing thoughts or panic, and perform better. We therefore:

- relax the body;
- relax the mind;
- let tension go.

First, it is important to take some time to learn to *detect* signs of tension. A simple way to do this is to tune in to all the signals and signs your body generates.

SENSORY AWARENESS TRAINING

We have already discussed how easy it is to ignore the messages that the body sends us. The following technique fosters an *increased* attention to the body, to aid in detecting and quieting physical tension.

Exercise one – paying attention

Sitting in a chair, let your right arm hang down. Now, place your left hand on the top of your right arm. Does it feel soft? Can you pinch the skin there? Now, raise your right arm slowly until it is level with your shoulder, and then keep it elevated and straight. Did you notice that as you began to lift the arm, the muscles became tense and hard? Keeping it up requires effort, and you may feel the muscles all over your arm tensing and contracting in order to keep your arm up. Can you pinch as much skin?

Continue to hold your arm out, but concentrate on the sensations from *within* the arm. As the muscles continue to work, you may notice that they feel warmer, and that little messages of effort or stiffness or soreness begin to come from muscles all down the arm. Pay close attention to these. What are they like? What words can you think of to describe them?

Now let your arm go. As it hangs by your side again, can you feel the muscles at the top of the arm become loose and relaxed? What about internally – what sensations do the muscles send as they relax?

Just rest for a few breaths, with both arms by your side.

Once again place your left hand on top of your right arm. Just picture raising your right arm – think the message 'raise'. Did you notice any movement?

Exercise two – passive awareness

Sit upright but relaxed in a chair. Do nothing but sit in the chair, slowing your breathing gradually until you are breathing slowly, deeply and calmly.

Now allow your attention to focus on your body where it touches the chair. Can you feel the surface of the chair through your shoulders, your back, your bottom and legs? Can you feel the material the chair is made of? Can you feel your own weight supported by the chair? Can you feel your body on the chair? Can you notice differences where you touch the chair lightly, and where you touch it heavily?

Exercise three – awareness at work

Notice how your body feels as you work through the day. On the half hour, stop what you are doing and concentrate on the sensations from your body. Scan your body from top to bottom, taking time to become aware of any tension or relaxation. Notice particularly the head/jaw/shoulders areas.

PROGRESSIVE BODY RELAXATION

This relaxation procedure is the one found on most reputable relaxation tapes. It was developed by Dr Edmund Jacobson as a way of demonstrating to patients their tension, and contrasting it with feelings of relaxation. This method has the advantage of showing you where you store tension in your body.

Learning to relax is a skill. You therefore need to practice it regularly. We can assure you confidently that with practice and repeated effort you can master this technique and experience the wonderful sense of calm and ease that it brings. It takes some time to complete, around 30–45 minutes, and is ideal for getting rid of tension at the end of the day and preparing you to get off to sleep.

There are very many books available that provide instruction on relaxation. Relaxation is a *doing* thing, however. We strongly urge you to consider joining a class that teaches relaxation, yoga or tai chi.

In order to do this exercise properly, you must:

- find a place free from interruptions or distractions;
- find a suitable time – relaxing is not as effective after a meal or heavy exercise;
- find a comfortable position – most people practice relaxation lying down;
- try not to force yourself to relax but *allow* relaxation to take over your body;
- not worry when your mind strays or you are distracted by noises. Don't do anything about it; just return gently and persistently to focusing on your body.

Relaxation Guidelines

Relaxation is closely tied to breathing. Co-ordinate your letting go with exhalations, and let your breath blow the tension away. Where we ask you to 'hold for a count', time it to about 5 slow heartbeats.

Talk these exercises into a tape recorder so you can play them back to yourself.

- Start by getting comfortable. If you wear contact lenses take them out; if you have tight or uncomfortable clothing loosen it; keep your legs and arms uncrossed.

- Begin to notice your breathing. Just be aware of your breath as it comes into your body and goes out again.

- Now allow your breathing to slow down and become deeper. Fill your lungs, producing movement in your lower abdomen. Use your diaphragm (chest) to breathe slowly, deeply and calmly.

- Do this for at least 5 breaths.

- Begin with your ankles. Focus your attention on your ankles and feet. Bend your feet up, pull them firmly towards you, and feel the tension in your ankle muscles as you do so.

- Note the signs of tightness or stiffness. Breathe out and relax the tension away. Let it go.

- Hold the feet up for 2 breaths, then let go, allowing all the tension to drain away from your feet and legs as you breathe out.

- Concentrate on the change that takes place as you let your ankle muscles relax. Notice whether they feel looser, warmer or heavier.
- Repeat the exercise, but this time push your feet away from you.
- Pause for a few breaths, doing nothing but allowing your body to relax.
- Now focus your attention on your calves and knees. Do not move any other part of your body.
- Straighten your legs and push your heels down against the floor. Feel the tension in your calves and the backs of your legs, and take note of what it feels like.
- Hold them like that for the space of 2 breaths, concentrating on the tension, then let go again. Just let your legs sink down and relax. Picture your leg muscles becoming loose and relaxed, tired and heavy, warm and still. Let go and do nothing.
- Repeat that exercise, this time pushing your legs *together* as hard as you can.

Repeat these tightening and relaxing exercises with all the major muscle groups. Use the following list to guide you and show you which muscles to exercise.

Feet and ankles	
Knees and thighs	
Buttocks and lower back	squeeze buttocks together; gently arch back
Stomach	tighten stomach; push stomach out
Chest	take a deep breath and hold for a count of at least 15, then exhale slowly
Shoulders	shrug up high and hold for a count of 15
Neck	do not rotate your neck! tip slowly to the left and hold for 5 beats; gently tip to the right and hold for 5 beats; point chin at ceiling and hold for 5 beats; lower chin to chest and hold for 5 beats

Arms and hands	hands into fists for 10 beats; spread fingers wide for 10 beats; stretch arms stiffly by side for 10 beats
Face	arch eyebrows in surprise; scrunch eyes tightly shut; open mouth wide; poke tongue out

RELAX THE MIND

It is surprising to many people that it is very hard to stop our thoughts and relax mentally, yet one of the most common requests from people who feel stressed is: 'I wish my mind would stop racing!'

Try this experiment. Close your eyes and do not think of an ice-cream cone.

Were you successful? Lots of people report having enormous trouble trying to *stop* themselves thinking about something they don't want to think about or find distressing. Mostly success comes from imagining something else altogether. Paradoxically, the act of trying *not* to think of something means you *must* think of it in order to not think about it! Some people also report a feeling of panic if they are successful in stopping intrusive or racing thoughts, as if they have somehow lost the sense of control they experienced when dwelling on troubled thoughts. We speculate that this type of thinking is a *habit*, and like many habits, helps create the sense of normal, routine life, even if that life involves lots of anxiety and worry.

Don't worry, however! It *is* possible to stop racing or intrusive thoughts, although it will require some practice and effort.

The way to stop unwanted thoughts seems paradoxical: *you stop trying to stop them.* Viktor Frankl, the psychiatrist whose work we met in chapter 5, first realised that allowing the thoughts to enter our mind without distress or attempting to force them away takes the 'sting' out of them, and they will naturally float away again. It seems to be the anxiety about *having* the thoughts which leads us to dwell on them. It is also important to realise that thoughts by themselves are not harmful; in fact most people entertain thoughts of suicide, or affairs, or leaving relationships, or killing their bosses at some point. We see thoughts as very different from actions. Giving yourself permission to have the occasional unwanted thought by saying, 'It's no big deal', may lead to the thoughts fading away entirely.

If you are interested in this area read a book by Dan Wegner with the wonderful title *White Bears and Other Unwanted Thoughts: Suppression, Obsession and the Psychology of Mental Control*, New York, Viking Books, 1989.

Do this by letting the thoughts come in and exit when they choose, without placing a value judgement on them and by remaining as calm as you can. Try saying, 'That's interesting', or even fake boredom: 'Oh, another worry thought. How tedious.'

The other way to slow down our minds is to entertain thoughts of calm, soothing or peaceful scenes. The following exercise is used by top athletes to calm themselves before international competitions, and many people report that it is helpful at work *before* a stressful encounter. It takes some practice, and you need to be familiar with noticing tension in the body and letting it go (see the progressive body relaxation exercise on p. 93), so persevere. It works by taking advantage of the body's tendency to follow the mind.

Relax the Mind Instructions
- Sit (or lie) comfortably.
- Breathe deeply, slowly and calmly.
- Think of a place that is very dear to you. This may be a holiday spot, a place you visited when you were a child, or even a favourite armchair at home. It does not really matter, except that you must feel safe there and know that you can relax, without worries, and be yourself.

- Imagine your special place as realistically as you can. What is the weather like? Are you sitting or lying down? What does the ground feel like? What noises do you hear? What colours stand out?

- Now relax. Enjoy this mini-holiday. If other thoughts come into your mind, do not block them, but allow them to drift out again as you gently return your focus to your scene.

- Imagine the expression on your face. See yourself smiling, at peace and calm.

- Feel your tension fading away. Notice how much more relaxed you feel every time you breathe out. Feel that you are drawing energy from your imaginary environment. Breathe the clean, fresh air and feel your worries melting away.

- Stay there for as long as it feels good. When you want to leave, slowly allow your scene to disappear, and gently come back to your real surroundings.

When you have become familiar with this technique, you can use it almost anywhere. Experiment by picturing your worries as clouds, and watch them drift higher and further away until they disappear over the horizon. Other visualisations include:

- sinking into a warm bath;
- feeling your tensions melt away.

Letting Tension Go

The key to this exercise is pairing breathing out and letting tension go. Use it before, during and after difficult situations – for example, while you are driving; before a tough interview with the boss; or after you have spent an hour typing files.

- Notice where your tension is. Are your hands gripping the wheel too tightly? Are your jaws or stomach clenched? Are your shoulders and neck stiff?

- Take a *deep*, easy breath. Breathe in – and in – and in. Now hold it for a slow count of 5.

- Breathe out with an audible sigh, letting your shoulders sag, your jaw loosen and your hands relax slightly. Feel the tension drain away.
- Continue to breathe slowly and calmly.
- Repeat this process, working through the major body parts described on page 95.

As you become more skilled at these exercises, you will find that, far from being tired, lethargic or sleepy, you will feel refreshed, invigorated and ready to go.

BREATHING AND RELAXATION

If you have ever watched a martial arts demonstration, you will be struck by the hissing, forceful breathing that accompanies action. This is a powerful demonstration of how breath control can be harnessed to invigorate and provide strength. Women who have given birth will also be well aware of how holding a breath while bearing down hard can give the mother strength during childbirth.

Observing someone who has just finished a job or task will also reveal how breathing out, or exhaling, signals the start of the let-down or relaxation response. Sighing often accompanies the end of effort or strain.

Try this exercise. Tighten all your muscles at once, as tight as you can make them, and hold it for a count of one, two… three. Now relax and let go.

You probably noticed that when you tightened your muscles you *held* your breath, and that when you let go and relaxed, your breath rushed out.

The link between exhalation and relaxation is useful to trigger relaxation whenever it is needed. The following exercises are guaranteed to reduce the level of your stress in minutes. Paired with calming images or thoughts, they are the first aid in stress management.

The 5 and 3 minute relaxations are easily performed most places, even at work. You can even do them in the loo if privacy is needed!

This exercise could be done in the car during a traffic jam or at the lights (leave your eyes open). It could also be done in the line at the supermarket or at a doctor's surgery or an airport.

Five-Minute Relaxation Through Breathing

- Sit still and upright in a chair. Close your eyes.

- Breathe calmly and normally. Notice and pay attention to your breathing. Listen to the sounds your breath makes as it comes into your body and goes out. Do this for 3 or 4 breaths.

- Now, turn your attention to the sensations you feel when you exhale. Don't think about breathing in, just let your body do that when it wants. On exhalation, many people report sensations of warmth, heaviness, sinking down, slowing down, letting go, breathing longer, slower or deeper, or feeling more comfortable or more relaxed.

- Stay focused on the sensation you notice most as you breathe out. Each time you exhale, feel that sensation affecting you more and more, spreading through your body. Do nothing but concentrate on breathing out and what it feels like.

- Continue in this way for 10 or 12 complete breaths.

- When you have felt the sensation for 10 or 12 breaths, simply stretch, open your eyes and take a deep breath, feeling calmer and more relaxed.

Gentle Three-Minute Breaths

Another very simple breathing exercise is simply to slow down the rate at which you breathe. Normally we breathe at around 15–20 breaths per minute (probably less for athletes and the very fit), and this figure rises when we are stressed.

This exercise aims to slow your breathing right down – aim for only 5 breaths or fewer per minute, a figure that will accompany very deep feelings of relaxation. It is very easy consciously to drop the normal rate to only 5 or fewer per minute, simply by monitoring your breathing and very slowly exhaling and inhaling, *just as if you are moving in slow motion.*

- Sit still and upright in a chair (or stand). Close your eyes.

- Breathe calmly and normally. Notice and pay attention to your breathing. Listen to the sounds your breath makes as it comes into your body and goes out. Do this for 3 or 4 breaths.

- Now, exhale to a slow count of 10, pause and inhale to a slow count of 10. Neither hold your breath nor force it out. The relaxation comes from slowing down the normal process.
- Continue for at least 20 breaths or until you feel calm and in control.

This exercise is an ideal one to do in tense situations.

Invigoration Through Breathing

We can apply the same principles of breath control to provide stimulation or energy when we are feeling tired or drained.

- Sit still and upright in a chair, or stand tall and straight.
- Focus your attention on how you feel. Breathing regularly and normally, turn your attention to the sensations you notice on breathing in. Many people report feelings of tension, alertness, coolness, expansion or tightening.
- Breathe in slightly deeper and faster than you did before. Concentrate on the sensations of inhalation; allow your body to exhale as it will.
- Continue for 4 or 5 breaths only, noticing all the time any changes in how you are feeling.
- Stretch and take a deep, deep breath in; open your eyes and exhale with a quick pant: 'Hhhuuhhh! Get going!'

Note that pairing a word to repeat in your mind as you do the exercise can greatly enhance the action of each of them. Thus, saying 'calm' or 'relax' when breathing out can aid in relaxation. Repeating a word like 'strong' or 'alert' whilst inhaling can also improve those sensations associated with the invigoration exercise.

The White Tornado

Dr Beata Jencks developed methods of imaging to augment the exercises above. This is one of her methods for invigoration:

- On inhalation, imagine your breath swirling into a cool, white tornado that whirls through your head. It sweeps up tiredness and the cobwebs of fatigue.

Beata wrote a number of books and articles and was an important, influential teacher. Read her book *Your Body: Biofeedback at its Best*, Chicago, Nelson and Hall, 1977.

- On exhalation, imagine the tornado moving rapidly down through your body and exiting through your navel.

- Repeat several times, ending on a deep inhalation followed by a quick release.

THE RELAXATION CONTRACT

The benefits of relaxation are noticed quite quickly. However, research has shown that many people give up their practice once their stress has dropped. This is understandable. Many of us find it a hassle to have to do something when we are tired or irritable, even if it is beneficial. It is easier to put up with the hassle and stress, or to take something to relieve it – alcohol, pain killers, drugs or food. But the effects of relaxation and other techniques like meditation persist only if *we* persist.

We have therefore included a contract that will help you both to monitor your relaxation and progress and to establish some rewards for keeping on going. When you run out of this contract, let's hope the relaxation response is a habit!

First rate your overall daily tension or stress level for a week before starting, using the scale below.

1	2	3	4	5	6	7	8	9	10
calm and relaxed				tense			uptight		stressed!

Then do the same thing each day of your relaxation weeks. You should see your ratings drop steadily and stay low.

PHYSICAL RELAXATION

Week	Sunday	Monday	Tuesday	Wednesday	Thursday	Friday	Saturday
baseline	Tension today	Tension today	Tension today	Tension today	Tension today	Tension today	Tension today
1	Practice yes/no Tension today	Practice yes/no Tension today	Practice yes/no Tension today	Practice yes/no Tension today	Practice yes/no Tension today	Practice yes/no Tension today	Practice yes/no Tension today
2	Practice yes/no Tension today	Practice yes/no Tension today	Practice yes/no Tension today	Practice yes/no Tension today	Practice yes/no Tension today	Practice yes/no Tension today	Practice yes/no Tension today
3	Practice yes/no Tension today	Practice yes/no Tension today	Practice yes/no Tension today	Practice yes/no Tension today	Practice yes/no Tension today	Practice yes/no Tension today	Practice yes/no Tension today
4	Practice yes/no Tension today	Practice yes/no Tension today	Practice yes/no Tension today	Practice yes/no Tension today	Practice yes/no Tension today	Practice yes/no Tension today	Practice yes/no Tension today

At the end of every week I will check with my friend

_____

Once they have confirmed that I have indeed practiced diligently, I am allowed to reward myself with

_____

(a pleasant food, drink or activity).

Signed _____

Witnessed _____

We have suggested having another person involved because we have learned that making a public commitment has a much stronger influence on behaviour than the deals we do 'in our heads'.

Lots of luck.

CHAPTER 8

Dealing with strong feelings

In chapter 6 there was a brief description of the work of American psychologist James Pennebaker, who has examined both the health costs of repressing negative emotions and the benefits of disclosing them in some way.

In Pennebaker's early experiments at Southern Methodist University in Texas he encouraged students to write about either a neutral subject (how they spent their holidays) or matters of deep personal concern. Comparing the two groups over the next year, Pennebaker found that the students who wrote about their deepest thoughts and feelings visited the campus medical service less often than the other students – they got sick less often. This effect held even after just one week of writing! This is a remarkable finding. In more sophisticated experiments Pennebaker and many other researchers have confirmed that repressing negative and hostile thoughts, memories and feelings is injurious to our health. Conversely, it seems that there are positive benefits from disclosing thoughts and emotions.

This lends strong support for the benefits of the so-called talking cures, like psychotherapy and counselling, as a method for relieving feelings of distress. The work of Pennebaker and others is important because psychotherapy is a very hard treatment to measure. Interestingly, Martin Seligman, whom we mentioned earlier, was a notable critic of the efficacy of psychotherapy, but he has recently changed his mind in favour of counselling as a result of a very large public survey he helped an American consumer organisation conduct.

Why should disclosure have such a powerful beneficial effect? The likely explanation is that the act of holding back or sitting on thoughts takes work and effort, and that letting go brings release from effort. It is also likely that writing down our feelings and getting them out of our head helps bring order and understanding. Instead of trying to hang on to the totality of the experience, small parts and pieces can be seen for what they are. Then, too, writing involves telling a story: it may be that the narrative through time helps us reach a sense of perspective.

Martin Seligman, *The Effectiveness of Psychotherapy. The Consumer Reports study* (1995). American Psychologist, 50, 965-974.

So how can you tap into the healthful benefits of discharging negative emotions and thoughts? The following method is useful.

THE DAILY JOURNAL

A journal offers a chance both to focus on our experiences and to reflect upon them. That in turn allows us to consider courses of action, regain our centre of balance and place the event in the context in our lives.

James Pennebaker, *Opening Up*, New York, Avon Books, 1990.

Pennebaker offers the following advice for journal writing:

- Explore both what is happening for you and how you feel about it. Let go – write about your deepest emotions and feelings.
- Write continuously. If you 'block', just rewrite what you have written.
- Three don'ts: don't judge what you write as you do it; don't intellectualise (quoting from Wittgenstein may impress the neighbours but won't improve your health); and don't use writing as an excuse for uncensored complaining.

We have developed the short acronym HERO to help you structure your journal as you are getting started. As you become more confident, we are sure you will fall naturally into your own style. Be careful, it's infectious!

H What is *Happening* for you? Describe the situations that are causing you upset or stress (or pleasure). Don't limit yourself to the present if it is an old worry that persists.

E What is the *Emotion* that comes from this? How are you feeling? What thoughts flow into your mind and what feelings do you experience? Just write in a flow – let out whatever comes, without holding back or censoring yourself.

R *Reflect* on what you have written and are thinking and feeling – read back through what you have written. Are you using writing as a substitute for action?

O *Open* yourself up to the implications of this event. What point does this event have in the context of your life? What meaning does it have for you? Do you detect themes or patterns around this event – has something like this occurred in your life before? When will there be an end to it? Can you see a way to bring this event to a close? Where to from here – what is your next step? What will you do to move yourself forward?

If writing is hard for you, Pennebaker suggests trying the 'talking cure' – disclosing what is going on for you into a cassette recorder. Again, don't censor your words: just allow your thoughts to flow in a stream of words.

Disclosing to friends, family and lovers can have the same result although, surprisingly, many people find this harder to do than to write in a journal.

There are times, of course, when it is helpful or even necessary to talk to others about what is happening to you. See chapter 10 for ideas about seeking professional resources.

DEALING WITH LOSS (AND WINNING THE LOTTERY)

One of the special circumstances in which issues about disclosure and withholding thoughts are brought into sharp focus is when we lose something of value, or when someone we love dies. Let's take some time to examine this in more detail.

'I won Lotto!' cried a client of ours some time ago. The fantasy of achieving such a dream certainly keeps many people buying tickets regularly. We all imagine what we would do with our riches and how our lives would change: no more work and drudgery, and lots more holidays, travel, clothes, cars and fun.

The cry of this client was not one of joy, however, but one of despair and frustration – he had won Lotto but he had lost his old life and friends and habits. Turning down requests for gifts and loans had caused offence to friends. Buying a new house, car and clothes caused jealousy. Going to restaurants and visiting Pacific Island resorts meant no one in his old crowd could possibly come too. Although the win brought many nice new things, it occasioned a period of transition that meant loss, change and much painful growth.

In many ways that is what life is about – endings and transitions and beginnings. Several writers have described the developmental stages that people pass through in growing up, leaving home, being adult, producing children, entering old age, burying parents, facing our own decline and death. Each of these brings stress in one form or another, whether we recognise it or not. Change requires us to cope and adapt, and that inevitably leads to stress.

Physical symptoms in people who have suffered a loss of some kind are all reminiscent of the stress symptoms described earlier in this book: lack of appetite, sleeplessness, knots in stomach, shaky legs, headaches, an inability to concentrate and depression are all familiar. Psychological consequences can include feelings of disbelief, shock, numbness, guilt, blame, sheer panic, anguish, waves of sadness, anxiety, hopelessness and short-term memory loss. Longer-term consequences might include confusion, anger, fear of losing control, relief, lowered self-esteem, a sense of isolation, loneliness, helplessness, sadness, feeling like a piece of yourself has gone, and despair.

Our belief is that all change, no matter how slight, involves some loss and some grieving. To explore the notion of stress and loss we want to concentrate on the death of a loved one. The discussion and advice could apply to many situations, such as redundancy, divorce or even aging.

Death, Dying and Grieving

There really isn't any way to write about grieving that makes the process less painful to experience or read about. In our work with people who are grieving the loss of someone close, the most frequently asked question we hear is, often more than a year after the event: 'Am I normal? My friends (or family, or colleagues) have said I should be over it and shaping up and carrying on.'

The answer is that there is no proper time frame for getting over a loss. For a few the loss will never really pass. When parents lose a child, or a person loses a partner after many years together, everything changes for ever. Dreams are changed, and attitudes, values and a sense of belonging are permanently altered.

But what happens when we don't permit ourselves to grieve or we notice that someone we love has not been grieving over their loss? Research shows that if we do not grieve we usually cannot live life to the fullest, and often experience feelings of shame, guilt and ongoing suffering. Our personal experience matches what we have seen from our clients and from evidence from research studies: opening up, accepting the loss and integrating it into our lives leads to speedier recovery, better health and emotional wellbeing.

Ann Kaiser Stearns interviewed people four years after the death of someone they loved. She found that those who went on to regain a rewarding and fully functioning life had to undertake lots of personal growth and learning. The people who coped best held themselves open to what occurred and did not shut it away. This bears out the findings from the work of James Pennebaker and also our secrets of people who cope well on pages 54-67.

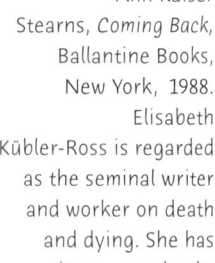

Ann Kaiser Stearns, *Coming Back*, Ballantine Books, New York, 1988. Elisabeth Kübler-Ross is regarded as the seminal writer and worker on death and dying. She has written many books which are commonly available.

Elisabeth Kübler-Ross, the renowned teacher and researcher, identified two important components in recovery from loss: intellectual and emotional resolution.

Intellectual resolution involves making sense of the event, trying to understand why the loss happened, how it happened, what lessons we needed to learn from it, and how to move away from the pain.

Emotional resolution is usually the harder to achieve and takes much much longer. It involves resolving an 'identity change'. The identity change means we can neither remain the person we once were nor view ourselves in the same way. As Stearns says, 'In order to go forward it is necessary to integrate the changes that have transpired into our daily activities': our philosophy of life, our relationship with others and our approach to the future. Recovery means accepting our changed circumstances in order once again to find pleasure in life and something to live for.

Stages of Grieving

Elisabeth Kübler-Ross describes the normal stages that we go through when we lose a loved one. These stages are fluid. The feelings may replace each other within the same hour; they may exist side by side, and they may come and go at will, without our having much control over them. The common stages are:

1 *Denial and isolation*, as if we are saying, 'No, it can't be'.

2 *Anger, resentment, rage, envy*. Sometimes this stage is repressed, because we feel ashamed of our feelings. One client of ours felt jealous because all her friends had babies while she was unable to conceive; another was furious because the wife of a friend was alive and healthy even though she was a smoker, while his wife had died of lung cancer.

3 *Bargaining or the attempt to postpone*. This is sometimes helpful for brief periods of time. As one client said, 'If only you let my teenager return safely this evening, I promise I will start going to church regularly', or 'I promise I will never fight with my husband again if you just make him well again'.

4 *Depression*. We can no longer deny our loved one's illness or death. We usually have what is called (i) a reactive depression and (ii) a preparatory depression. Reactive depression is a normal reaction to what is going on; preparatory depression takes into account what is happening or is about to happen. This sad stage is necessary to absorb the *reality* of what is occurring.

5 *Acceptance*. This stage is almost devoid of feeling, as if the pain is gone, and for some people interest in activities or people diminishes. This period is one in which a great deal of psychological growth can occur. When a client of ours was dying,

we noticed outside interests held less interest as the person became ready within himself for his own death.

It seems to us that people in society are slowly learning to talk about death and dying as a normal and intricate part of life. As this becomes more acceptable we find more and more people able to talk through their feelings of having loved ones die, or of losses of all kinds. Through doing this important talking we develop more accepting, open attitudes to loss and death.

The best gift we can give someone who is dying is to sit quietly and encourage their talking, and to listen and to hear when they are ready and have accepted their own death. It is important for those of us who continue living to listen to where the dying person is at rather than to convey our wish to try to keep the person alive at all costs.

Beginnings of Recovery

In coping with a loss it is important for us to be gentle with ourselves. Stearns notes that a lot of energy is used for healing and there will be little energy left to reach outward at the moment. A lot of people in our lives want to be helpful and give all sorts of good suggestions, like, 'If you feel like crying, do so'. She suggests choosing the ideas that appeal to you, and let go of the ones that don't.

- The body needs energy for repair. Don't rush too much, and go gently on yourself. Be patient with yourself. Healing takes a long time.

- Do not take on new responsibility right away. Keep decision-making to a minimum and do not overextend yourself.

- Accept help and support when offered. Ask for help. Family and friends cannot read our minds; it is OK to need comforting. Rest and more rest.

- Seek support of others; visit friends, relatives, and invite someone over. If you are going through very difficult times, stick to activities which you find particularly comforting.

- Lean into the pain; it cannot be outrun. Let the healing process run its full course.

- Remember it is OK to feel depressed. It is good to cry. You feel better afterwards.

- Read. There are many helpful books on grief: the more you understand it, the easier it becomes to handle. There are also books for children to help with loss too.

- Good nutrition is important to help the healing process. Moderate exercise, such as walking, is helpful.

- Keep a journal. It is a good way to understand what you are feeling and thinking. Take quotes that are helpful to you and post them where you can see them.

- Plan new interests. Plan things to look forward to – trips, visits, lunch, etc. Learn or do something new, or rediscover old interests, activities and friends.

- Balance your life – read, rest, work.

Do's and Don't's in Helping Others With Loss

We are often asked about how to help people who are grieving. It is often hard to know what to say, and difficult to judge when to offer practical help or to stand back and give them space. Below is the distillation of our experience and readings.

DO'S

- Read about the stages of grief and the grieving process. Kübler-Ross's classic book *On Death and Dying* is highly recommended.

- Understand that the stages are never ordered. It will almost always take longer than you think it 'should'.

- Offer a squeeze of the hand, a hug, a kiss. Let the person know you care.

- Talk about good memories; they help healing.

- Let the person be wherever they are with their emotions at that moment.

- Connect with that person when you really can hear and have the time to listen.

- Offer a cup of coffee, write a note, visit, bring food, give a pertinent book, offer to help in ways that you can follow through on.

- Remember that a person who can stay through this process with another person is a very precious and valuable friend indeed.

DON'TS

- Say 'You will get over it in time'. Time will soften the hurt but 'getting over it' diminishes the value of the loss.

- Say 'You will be better off without him' or 'It is God's will', as these are often not very consoling.

- Assume that the person does not want to talk about the loss. Check it out with the person directly.

- Give a pep talk. Remember there is no timetable for the end of a grieving process.

- Get discouraged and abandon that person. Strong negative feelings are a normal part of this process and healing cannot begin without all the emotions being allowed to surface and be accepted.

If you are not sure of what to do, ask the person directly, 'How can I help?'

Strong feelings are just that – feelings. In our experience it doesn't mean that people are obliged to act on them, and in fact for most it just means 'This is how I'm feeling now – will you listen?'

CHAPTER 9

The CALM approach

One of the best ways to deal with stress is to take an active, problem-solving approach to those issues that can be dealt with.

This chapter takes you through a straightforward process that identifies stresses in your life and then breaks them down into manageable chunks. The process can take some time, so plan on at least an hour or more that will be free from interruptions or distractions.

STRESS MAPPING

It may be useful to do this exercise with someone who knows you and your situation well, but you can certainly work through it by yourself if you want the privacy.

Take a big sheet of paper. Think about where in your life you feel the most pressure coming from. Start simply by brainstorming the areas where you feel pressured. Write them in the middle of the sheet.

The picture below suggests some areas to guide you, but do not be limited by these. Do not censor your writing at all – remember that writing can in itself act as a stress release (see chapter 8 for more information about the effects of disclosure). Just take the time to get *all* your concerns and pressures out of your head and into the light of day.

Doing this will not make them any worse!

While you think of the pressures on you, make sure you have in mind a specific, concrete example to demonstrate how the stress is caused.

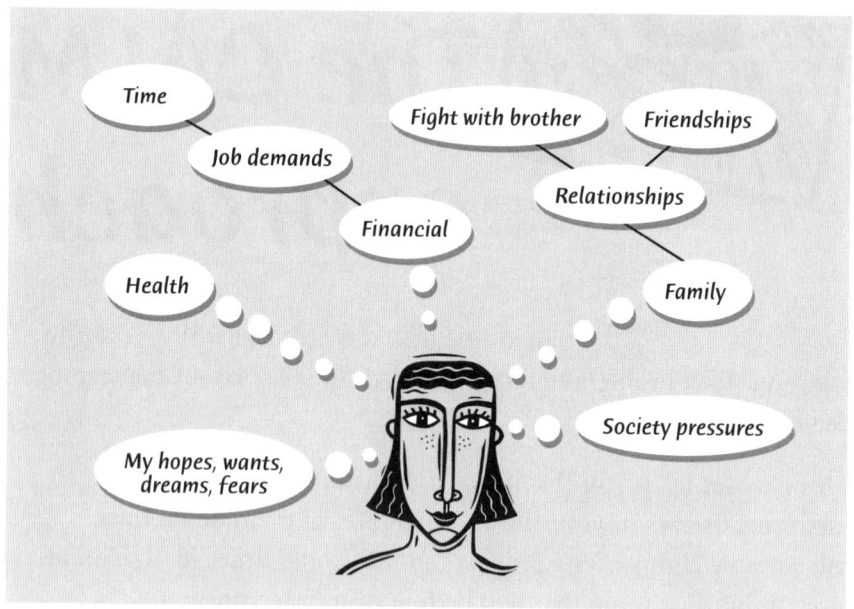

Once you have written down all your current concerns and worries, STOP!

Take a five-minute break. Do some stretches, make a cup of tea or just stare out the window for a while.

Now write down the specific examples you had in mind during your brainstorming, plus the 'add-on' stresses that emerge from each area, as we've done below. Just follow the 'flow' of your thoughts, as if you were talking to yourself. Ask yourself how each stressor causes you stress. Take your time and try to map your stress in as much detail as you can.

You can also take the opportunity to express just how each one feels to you. Use different coloured pens to describe the level of feeling.

Add drawings of the stress – what does it look like?

For example, Brent mapped the stress he was feeling around his work. The first thing he thought of was the accountant Marie. Brent thinks Marie has an 'attitude' – for example, Marie complained to the boss about Brent without confronting him directly. Brent also thinks Marie is dictatorial in her management, often over petty things, such as telling a colleague to change her pen colour, but also in setting unreasonable deadlines. These things cause Brent to feel angry and hostile towards Marie – but unable to do much because of the status and power difference between them.

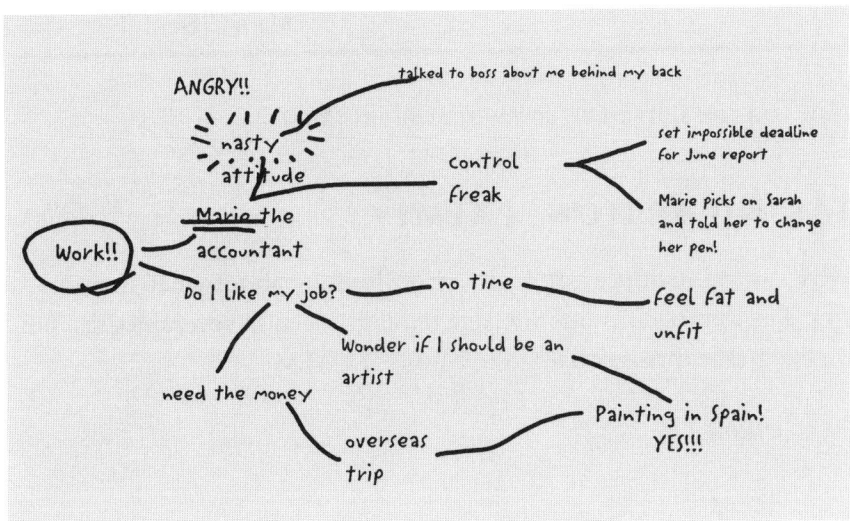

The other thing that stressed Brent out about work was his wondering whether he should be in this job at all. His heart tells him he should be a full-time artist. But he needs the job to get the money for a trip to Spain to try 4 months of full-time painting!

Ranking

Now go through your big stress map and rank the stressors that cause you most upset, with 1 being the most stressful. Then write out this list again, with examples. Then consider it carefully. Can you *rank* all these pressures from most stressful to least stressful, as we have for Brent?

Rank	Pressure	Feelings	Specific example
1	MARIE	anger frustration	talked behind my back sets tight deadlines
2	painting	despair	will I ever paint full time?
3	money	gloom	saving seems slow blew $275 on Doc Marten shoes
4	feel fat and unfit	embarrassed pissed off at me	haven't exercised in two weeks worked late instead on Marie's report

Now you can start to do something about them.

TAKING ACTION, CALMLY

We want to introduce you to a way of thinking about what stresses you. The approach is one we have regularly seen in several forms, but we like best expressed using the acronym CALM:

Change

Accept

Let go

Manage

The emphasis in CALM is on being active in changing our situation in as creative and healthy manner as we can. It is far better to be vigorous in shaping our own lives. The *Change* and *Manage* parts of the technique emphasise the active. But there are circumstances and situations we can never *change* – the death of a family member perhaps, or even an unjust act visited upon us by a co-worker. The *Accept* and *Let go* parts of CALM emphasise learning to live with situations, or letting go of some of our precious assumptions or hopes.

If, for example, Brent continues to spend money (like $275 on shoes) he must accept that feeling annoyed with work because he is not yet painting in Spain *is his responsibility*. He will need to change some of his ways with money to fix that situation – or learn to live with his frustrating job.

What in your situation is open to creative change?

CHANGE
What can you change about this situation:
circumstances;
time frames;
other people's expectations;
requirements or resources;
your thoughts or feelings?

Once you have identified these things, there may need to be some acceptance of things that can't be changed.

ACCEPT
that not everything is available to be changed;
that things will not always work out;
that you cannot be perfect, please everyone or be 100%;
that life owes you nothing.

To do the work of accepting that not everything can be changed, you may have to let go of some of your feelings.

LET GO
If you have changed what you can, done the best you can do, then you may need to let go of some worries, concerns, fears, guilt or anxiety.

Think of this as having a psychological clean-out. Just as you wouldn't move to a new house with all the rubbish left over from your old one, neither can you move forward in life if you continually lug all the baggage of grudges, slights and hurts from the past. What then is left? *You, of course.*

MANAGE
this situation the best you can:
your reactions;
thoughts;
feelings; and
your resources.

If nothing else in a situation can be managed, you always have the ability to manage your own reactions and thoughts. You are free to behave as you wish. Can you behave in a healthy, affirming way, no matter what the situation? It is up to you.

CALM IN ACTION

To implement the CALM approach, let's put Brent's stressors through the process below:

1   *Take the list of all current areas of stress:*

   1   Marie's deadlines

   2   Marie's behaviour

   3   My money concerns

   4   I'm unfit and feel fat

2   *Now divide the list items into 3 categories:*

   1   Stress that can be fixed by thought and effort

   2   Stressors that may be fixable, but may have to be endured

   3   Stressors that will not go away or are outside of your control and that require you to cope or survive

Still using the example of Brent, we have worked through a range of possibilities to identify where he needs to apply effort, and where he may be wasting effort or emotional energy.

A) Stress that requires action (stress that is definitely avoidable)

Questions to ask of yourself:

> *What do I need to do? What's my plan? What resources or help do I need? Who can help? What's my time frame?*

In Brent's case:

1 *Money concerns*

> I have to develop a budget.
>
> Maybe I can put a deposit on the trip to get me committed.
>
> I need to review my spending.

2 *I'm unfit*

> Start using my gym membership.
>
> Get involved in the company cricket team.
>
> Walk to work.

3 *Marie's deadlines*

> Ask her for a change.
>
> Get more notice of the time frame.
>
> Ask what she expects.

B) Stress that needs information or clarity (stress that may or may not be avoidable)

Questions to ask:

> *Tell me more? What reasons? For example? How long? Where? Suggested changes? All the time? Who has responsibility?*

In Brent's case:

1 *Marie's behaviour*

> Marie's behaviour doesn't make sense to me. What do I need to learn to understand better?
>
> I need to find out if she acts this way with others.
>
> I may need to approach her directly and see if she has a problem

with me.

I may need to examine my own behaviour.

C) Stress that calls for a new attitude or philosophy (stress that is definitely unavoidable and must be endured or coped with)

Questions to ask:

How will I cope? What will I do differently? How can I manage myself? How can I view this differently? What must I do to live with this?

In Brent's case:

1 *Marie's deadlines (if she will not accommodate any change)*

   I'm stuck with this – how can I cope without getting steamed?

   Marie isn't going to change – worrying and getting stressed out won't affect anyone but me. I'm better to pour my energy into some positive action for myself.

   What is the worst thing that could happen anyway, even if I miss one deadline?

   Maybe I have to say I can't deliver – is that so bad?

   I just have to put up with this for another 8 months, then I'm off to Spain!

2 *Money concerns*

   Although I want to wear new clothes, I want to paint more.

   Every artist has to struggle sometime, so I'd better learn how now!

   I can either earn more or want less – what's my choice?

See chapter 6 for help with self-talk.

Notice how Brent has used self-talk to help change his attitude. Often we place ourselves under stress by holding on to ways we think people should behave. But who said they have to do what we want? Changing our thoughts can and does have a profound effect on how we feel.

List your own concerns here:

Rank	Pressure	Feelings	Specific example
1			
2			
3			
4			
5			
6			
7			

A) Stress that requires action (stress that is avoidable)

Questions to ask:

> *What do I need to do? What's my plan? What resources or help do I need? Who can help? What's my time frame?*

1) _____
2) _____
3) _____
4) _____

B) Stress that needs information or clarity (avoidable-unavoidable)

Questions to ask:

> *Tell me more? What reasons? For example? How long? Where? Suggested changes? All the time? Who has responsibility?*

1) _____

2) _____

3) _____

4) _____

C) Stress that calls for a new attitude or philosophy (unavoidable)

Questions to ask:

> *How will I cope? What will I do differently? How can I manage myself? How can I view this differently? What must I do to live with this?*

1) _____

2) _____

3) _____

4) _____

THE FILOFAX TECHNIQUE

In working with many clients who have had difficulties dealing with stress, we have been impressed by some of the creative ways in which they have managed to change or adapt their lives. The example below was from a busy woman who found it hard to make time for herself and her family. So she set about adapting some of her Type A efficiency to work for her own good, and she began to schedule good times for herself in her diary. Initially, we thought this a bit obsessive, but the technique has since proved its worth again and again with others (and we even admit to using it ourselves).

Mapping out in advance your personal fun times, quiet times or down times will allow you to develop a sense of order and routine that can reduce the stress of 'unexpected' events. It will also allow you to establish priorities and set limits, so you can clearly see where important personal events are, and plan work around them. Or, if you suffer from never quite getting on to doing things, it will help by stimulating you to take some action.

The mere fact of looking forward to an outing or event can also be helpful in promoting a more optimistic frame of mind. You may even find yourself counting down to a scheduled occasion, just as children tend to do in the lead-up to holidays and birthdays ('How many sleeps until… ?').

Remember the Archangel exercise on page 64? Are you making the time for the things you said were meaningful to you?

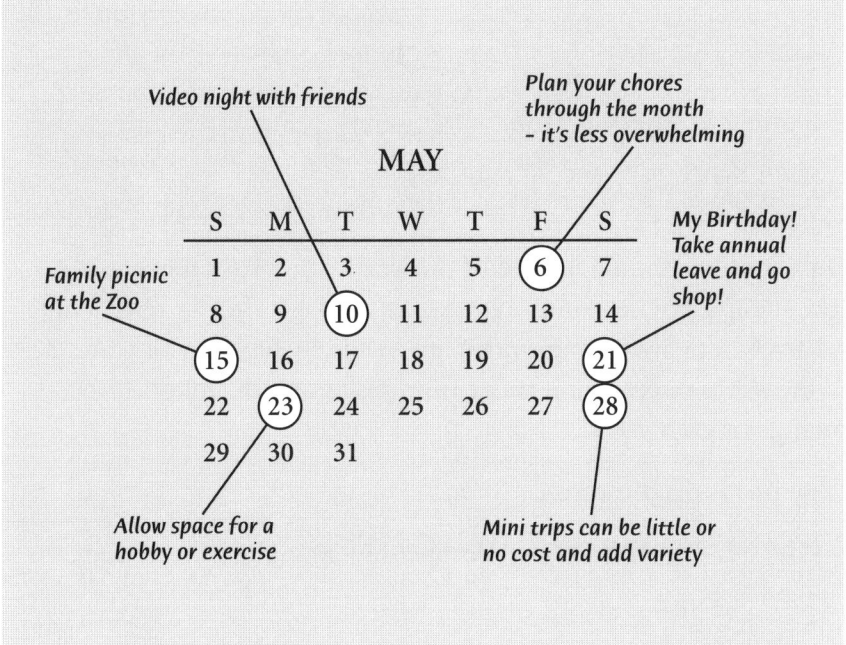

Planning life can help ensure you have free time and psychological space built in. Make sure you don't plan so much on weekends that it looks and feels like work!

STRESS-FREE SLEEP

Another side-effect of stress is difficulty getting to sleep or staying asleep. It's a nightmare! Lying there, tossing and turning, the mind full of thoughts, worries, lists, problems, that horrible feeling that you can't escape from it, that all you want is for your consciousness to stop. And then you know that if you don't sleep you'll feel more stressed in the morning, tired and grumpy and out of sorts… Oh for a sleeping pill.

Here is another problem that will respond to the CALM approach. There are a number of specific things you *can* change, and some others that will easily respond to being managed.

> There have been no documented cases of non-brain-injured people who never sleep, although many believe that they haven't slept a wink. Healthy adults sleep an *average* of 7.5 hours per night, and nearly 70% of the population sleep between 6.5 and 8.5 hours nightly. Teenagers seem to need more, possibly up to 10 hours a night, in order to cope with hormonal and growth changes (or at least that's what they will tell you when you need the chores done). If you live to be 75 years old, you will have spent between 18 and 25 years asleep.

On any one night, up to 20% of the world's population may suffer from temporary insomnia – an absolutely staggering number. While relatively rare bouts of insomnia are irritating, between 14% and 30% of the world's population suffer from insomnia which lasts for weeks, months or even years.

Insomnia is diagnosed only when:

- there is difficulty falling asleep within 30 minutes of retiring; and/or

- there are numerous awakenings during the night; and/or

- you wake during the night and take longer than 30 minutes to fall asleep again; and/or

- you wake more than 1 hour before your desired and regular rising time; *and*

- you are distressed by your difficulty and it has persisted longer than 3 weeks.

Self-Help for Sleeping Problems

From time to time we all suffer sleepless nights, especially as we get older. On such occasions we may simply need to be more accepting and let go of our anxiety about not sleeping.

It is very important for people with more chronic sleep problems to be regular about their night-time routine. The aim is for the end of your day to provide a number of signals, or cues, that *you are now entering the time for sleeping* (and only sleeping!). Many traditional night-time activities (such as reading in bed, or watching TV, or eating) may actually worsen your difficulty. The exception is sexual activity which generally promotes relaxation and sleep.

The guidelines below help you train your body and mind that the bedroom, and especially the bed, are triggers for sleeping.

To prepare yourself for sleep, start a wind-down ritual before entering the bedroom, and clear your worries and 'what ifs' from your mind before you retire for the night.

1. Lie down with the intention of going to sleep *only* when you are sleepy. Snuggle into your usual sleep position.

2. Always awaken *and* get up at the same time every morning. Don't be tempted to sleep 1 or 2 hours more after a wakeful night.

3. Try to establish and maintain a regular night-time routine. If possible, go to bed at the same time each night. Do not attempt to 'recover' lost sleep by retiring at 7pm – rest is a result of regular sleep patterns.

4. Avoid having naps during the day – this may make you more wakeful at night.

5. Try to make your bedroom, and especially your bed, a trigger for sleeping. Avoid non-sleep activities in the bedroom – this includes reading, TV, eating, etc. Never sleep anywhere but your own bed when at home.

6. Some people find light reading relaxing before bed. Avoid thrillers, horror stories or very stimulating books – and the same for TV and other stimulating activities. In general, wind down your activities before bed-time.

7. A warm (not hot) bath or shower relaxes you by increasing peripheral blood flow in the body. Avoid exercise last thing at night.

8. A hot milk drink (not coffee, tea, or chocolate drinks which contain caffeine) contains tryptanol, a naturally occurring mild sedative, and can be very effective. Make sure you have finished it 30–40 minutes before retiring.

9   Learn to use relaxation procedures upon retiring. Listen to a tape (that turns itself off) or mentally rehearse the procedures so that *you* condition your body to associate the feeling of relaxation with sleep.

10 If you cannot sleep after 30 minutes, or after awakening, leave your bed and go to another part of the house. Read the paper, listen to the radio, have a drink of milk, or engage in non-stimulating activity. Go back to your room when you are feeling drowsy. On returning, use relaxation techniques if you need to. Snuggle back into your usual sleep position and start this process again.

11 Mentally relax as well: imagine a peaceful, pleasant and relaxing scene. If you notice your thoughts racing, 'shift' them to your scene.

12 Use a journal to record thoughts and things to be done the next day. Don't allow your bed to become the one place in which you have the space to solve all your problems and worries!

QUIET ZONES AND ROUTINE

Our last CALM example was again demonstrated to us by a client. She provided us with a description of the sort of stress that millions of people face daily. She spoke of feeling as if there was never a time when, or a place where, she could let go and relax. As a mother and a wife she felt her time was always being allocated to others. Her children needed her from the moment they woke up; her husband felt that because he was working outside the home it was her job to keep the house clean and tidy, have meals cooked and keep the kids out of his hair. She also worked part-time looking after some of her neighbour's children for three afternoons a week. She began to feel desperate, as if there was never a time for her to let go.

While she worked with us on aspects of her situation, like dealing with her unco-operative husband, we suggested an idea to get a little space and time to herself – a completely private quiet zone.

The idea behind a quiet zone is that you can create a space for yourself that is yours alone and will always reflect feelings of calm, peace, quiet and tranquillity. Virginia Woolf termed it 'a room of one's own', or a sanctuary. The place you choose will act as a trigger for letting go of stress, worries and tension, even if just for 5 minutes.

Our client chose the bathroom, because it had a lock on the door. When the kids had gone to bed, she would run a bath, lock the door and soak for 20 minutes. She practiced deep breathing and letting go there, just enjoying the solitude and silence. She reported that the bathroom began to take on a special meaning for her – at times during the day she would retreat there for 5 minutes and let the calm wash over her.

This place need not be an entire room. It might be a favourite chair, a sunny spot under a window, a spot on a hill, perhaps the reading room in your public library or the peaceful, calming atmosphere of a church.

Once in your space, do nothing, do not solve problems and don't perform exercises; rather, let go of tension and just enjoy the chance to relax.

Try to ensure your quiet zone:

- remains undisturbed for as long as you need it;
- stays reasonably constant in feel and look;
- is easily accessible to you;
- is respected by others close to you at work or home.

Quiet Zones at Work?

Consider this – would you be more likely to interrupt someone who was staring into space or someone scribbling furiously at their desk?

Most people will interrupt the person 'doing nothing'. But what if they were reflecting and thinking deeply? Somehow we have associated rush and activity with 'real work', while we value stillness and reflection less.

The idea of quiet zones at work is not new. A firm of Canadian architects established a tradition at their offices of a two-hour quiet time in the afternoon when no one spoke (unless they had to); the answerphone was turned on and no meetings were allowed. This scheme was specifically designed to allow the architects room to think, to dream and to imagine – an essential activity for good architects.

Likewise we advised a firm of bankers to create a room in which their investment staff could retire to think and reflect – as opposed to indulging in the frantic reaction which was the industry standard. The room quickly became a favoured spot for calm and thought – used mostly by the CEO.

If there is no place to achieve calm, then try to set some time each working day for stillness and reflection. Take 10 minutes to stop thinking about work and deadlines. Don't concentrate on anything but allowing yourself the chance to slow down, empty your mind and relax.

What would happen if Parliament did that!

The Value of Routine

Children are wonderful teachers. One of the things we have learned from our children is the value of predictability in life. Although we have seen that creativity, innovation and change are stimulating to human beings, there are times when we suffer too much of it. Children, for instance, seem very sensitive to changes in their surrounding. Taking children on holiday can result in a few nights of bedlam as they adjust to a new routine. It is as if their anchor to what is safe and comforting is adrift, and their behaviour becomes chaotic until they can re-establish the continuity of their lives, the ongoing flow of familiar things in the midst of new adventure and event. The same thing happens if a visitor comes to stay. Having a favourite aunt visit occasions later bedtimes and longer stories – and we all pay for it the next day with a tired, grumpy child demanding more time of the parents.

In order to help maintain that sense of continuity and sameness for our children, we bring elements of their ordinary life with them on holiday – teddy bears, tricycles, clothes, cutlery, pillows. The list of what children have to have is as long and as varied as there are parents to talk about it.

The corollary of this for adults is seen in such things as favourite clothes for relaxing; or hobbies like gardening, reading, collecting, building, working on cars and so on. When we engage in familiar routines of activity, the pattern and level of our thinking changes. We can utilise the automatic, unconscious habits of thought to calm down and relax.

Conversely, when routines end or change, we may feel uncomfortable or out of place. This explains why people who are newly retired and who no longer have the regular demands of work to place structure on their days may often experience difficulties adjusting to their new lives. Likewise sportspeople who retire find that giving up regular training and gym visits can be unsettling, even if they have longed for the time when they can stop the pain of training.

Think for a minute of those people who seem to emanate a sense of peace and calm. In our experience and research, these individuals will have beloved activities or hobbies which allow them to let go and lose themselves, and which are rewarding in their own right. What is crucial is that these are tasks which allows people to become totally absorbed. Such people have a rhythm or flow to their lives which helps establish a sense of order and stability.

Spending time with farmers or members of autonomous religious communities will quickly reveal that there is a time for all the things that need to be done, and that hurrying only contributes to less enjoyment and a poorer job.

Try to establish some order or routine in your life, and allow time either for doing some hobbies or tasks on a regular basis, or for regularly engaging in a 'wind-down' ritual, be it an evening walk, 10 minutes of weeding, watching the sunset, or knitting 30 rows.

CHAPTER 10

Where to from here?

Our values throughout the book have been clear. We want you to be active in changing your own situation and supplying the help you need. We believe that each of us has ultimate responsibility for our own health and happiness.

If you have tried the techniques and suggestions we have provided in this book and are still not feeling better, *don't worry*. Stress is unlikely to be the event that kills you off, but worrying that you are still stressed won't help. Reducing feelings and causes of stress is a long-term project for some people, especially if you have lots on your plate, or are trying to change ingrained habits of thought or behaviour. As well, some of us experience complicated feelings that will need other kinds of interventions to help sort out.

The important thing is to make a start. Doing nothing will ensure that exactly that will occur: nothing. Australian cartoonist and author Andrew Matthews put it well when he said, 'Wherever you are, it is the place to start. The effort you expend today does make a difference'.

Andrew Matthews, *Being Happy! A handbook to greater confidence and security*, Singapore, Media Masters, 1988.

So if you have trouble helping yourself, it may be appropriate to talk about outside sources of help or guidance. *In almost every community there are resources available to assist you.* Some will charge and some will provide services that are subsidised or even free.

WHERE TO FROM HERE?

Where do you find help?

In New Zealand, your first port of call may be Citizen Advice Bureaus. They are located in local phone books, and CAB workers have at their fingertips many community resources, training and learning courses, and the contacts for agencies that may provide further help. CABs offer this service free of charge.

In many parts of Australia, Community Health Centres provide useful services.

Most of the larger councils in Australia and New Zealand put out Community Directories. They contain all emergency/crisis contacts, and religious, sports, hobby and recreation organisations, as well as childcare, age-care, national and ethnic groups, health organisations, hospitals, home care, counselling and many other helpful organisations.

In addition, general practitioners (local doctors) are often knowledgeable about where to go for assistance. They are a good place to start if you wish to seek help from specialist counselling services.

People in Australia may find Dr Deborah Saltman's, *With a Little Help*, Choice Books, 1996, a useful guide to choosing and assessing counselling services.

Your first step is to ask yourself what kind of help do you think you need. Ask lots of questions, and see whether the service offered will meet your need. If not, do not hesitate to get another referral.

In seeking help we strongly suggest you use people who are trained and qualified professionals in their field. These individuals typically belong to professional bodies who demand adherence to a code of ethics or safe practice and may require their members to maintain basic levels of training to remain current. For example, if you wish to see a psychologist, seek someone who belongs to a professionally recognised body such as the Australian Psychological Society or the New Zealand College of Clinical Psychologists.

AFTERWORD

This book was written as a practical guide that requires people to practise simple, proven techniques to combat their own problems with feelings of stress. But we wish the book to work in very pragmatic ways; you can help us to improve it in future editions by taking the time to *write to us with suggestions for changes, or to tell us of your own experiences with overcoming stress*. With your permission, we may include your story as an example to share with others. We are especially interested in the experiences of younger people and teenagers, stories about work, of coping with trauma and loss.

As we end this book, we wish you much good luck on your quest for a happier life, happier relationships and new coping mechanisms to enable a more stress-free, full life.

David Winsborough and Kay Allen
Box 12 443
Thorndon, Wellington
New Zealand

email psycho@xtra.co.nz

INDEX

Acceptance
    part of CALM approach, 116
    stage of grieving, 109
Adrenaline, released as response to stress, 19, 23, 73
Alarm phase of stress response, 25
Alcohol and stress, 12, 34, 38, 102
Anatomy of an Illness, Cousins, 85
Anticipatory stress, 49
Antonovsky, *Heath, Stress and Coping*, 58
Archangel activity, 64, 123
Art of stress, 13
Athletic application of Yerkes-Dodson law, 21, 73
Awareness training, 92
A Weight off Your Mind, Tupling, 3

Balance, art of stress in attaining, 13
Beck, *Cognitive Therapy*, 72
Behavioural signs of stress, 30
Being Happy, Matthews, 130
Beliefs
    limiting, 74
    stress, about, 6
Benson, The Relaxation Response, 51
Blood flow, reduced as response to stress, 19
Body relaxation, 88
    progressive, 93
Brag file, 86
Brain, stress and, 41
Breathing
    changes as response to stress, 18, 29, 89
    relaxation and, 99
Brew, *Stress and Distress*, 48, 81
Bungy jumping, as example, 47

CALM approach, 113
Catastophising, 41, 68, 75
Changes
    part of CALM approach, 116
    response to stress, in, 15, 34
    thinking, in, 68
Chronic stress arousal, 25
Cognitive Therapy, Beck, 72
Cohen, Tyrell and Smith, research by, 38
Coherence, sense of, 58
Coming Back, Stearns, 108

Commitment, aspect of hardiness, 57
Comprehensible, view of world, 59
Conditions, impact of stress on wide range, 38
Coney, *Beware - Life will be the death of us*, 54
Conscious incompetence, 69
Constant stress, 25
Control
    aspect of hardiness, 57
    power of believing in, 67
Coping
    secrets, 54-67
    strategies, 12, 40, 56, 58, 60, 74
Coping with Change, McCormack, 64, 74
Cortex, high level thinking, 43, 47
Cousins, *Reflections on Healing and Regeneration*, 85
Cows, revenge of, 49
Cumulative, stress is, 24
Cunning confusers, 77
    disputing, 84

Daily journal, 105
Dangerous drivers, 74
    disputing, 82
Death and Dying, On, Kubler-Ross, 111
Death, dying and grieving, 108
Definition of stress, 10
Denial, 28, 109
Depression
    link to stress, 37, 38
    stage of grieving, 109
Diary, method of capturing thoughts, 79
Digestion, slowing in response to stress, 19
Disease, whether linked to stress, 32

Eating patterns and stress, 3
Eat Your Stress Away, Pierce, 3
Ekman,
    research by, 27
    Unmasking the Face, 28
Ellis, *Growth Through Reason*, 84
Emotional
    resolution, in recovery from loss, 108
    signs of stress, 30
Exercises
    archangel, 64

awareness at work, 93
breathing, 99
CALM, 121
coping, 59
defining stress, 8
describing the physical response, 16
HERO journal, 106
limiting beliefs, 78
passive awareness, 93
paying attention, 92
positive beliefs, 87
relaxation, 88, 90, 94
relaxation contract, 102
relax the mind, 97
signs of stress, 29
stress mapping, 113
thoughts, differences between low-level and clear, 47
workplace, cultural messages, 33
Exhaustion phase of stress response, 26

Falling Down, movie portrayal of too much stress, 22
Family Violence Commission report, 1
Fight or flight response, 19, 22, 23, 44
Filofax technique, 122
Flexibility, aspect of hardiness, 58
Frankl, *Man's Search for Meaning*, 10, 56, 97
Friedmann and DiMatteo, *Health Psychology*, 39
From *Paralysis to Fatigue*, Shorter, 55
Fromm, *To Have or To Be*, 63

Generalised reaction, stress as, 9
Grieving, 108
Growth Through Reason, Ellis, 84
Guide to using the less stress book, 3

Hardiness, 57
Healing and recovery, 110
Health
    conditions linked to stress, 37, 38
    consequences of stress, 32
    factors impinging on, 35
    mafia, 54
Health Psychology, Friedmann and DiMatteo, 39
Health, Stress and Coping, Antonovsky, 58
Heart disease, stress and the Type A personality, 39

Heart rate, increase as typical response, 18
Helping others with loss, 111
HERO, journal structure, 105
Holmes and Rahe, research by, 36
Humour, importance of, 85
Hysterical strength, response to stress, 24

Illness, as outcome of stress, 34
Immune response lowered, 26, 29
Instinctive response to stress, 16, 21
Intellectual resolution, in recovery from loss, 108
Invigoration through breathing, 101

Jacobson, relaxation procedure, 93
Jenks
    white tornado method of imaging, 101
    Your Body: Biofeedback at its Best, 101
Journal, daily, 105
Judging commentary, 76

Kenton, *10 Day De-Stress Plan*, 3
Kiroshi syndrome, 32
Kobasa, research by, 57
Kubler-Ross
    On Death and Dying, 111
    stages of grieving, 109

Laughter, healing effects of, 85
Laws
    Seesaw, 24
    Yerkes-Dodson, 21
Leakage, signs of, 27
Less Stress Book, guide to using, 3
Letting go
    part of CALM approach, 116
    tension, 90, 98
Levels of thinking, 69
Limbic system, low level thinking, 44, 47, 70
Long-term stress, 25
Loss
    dealing with, 106
    helping others, 111
Lynch, *The Broken Heart*, 36

Manageable, view of world, 59
Manage, part of CALM approach, 116
Man's Search for Meaning, Frankl, 10
Matthews, *Being Happy*, 130

McCormack, *Coping with Change*, 64, 74
Meaningful, view of world, 59
Mental rehearsal, 86
Mind, relaxation of, 96
Muscles, changes in response to stress, 18, 29
Muscular disorders, link to stress, 37
Myths and misconceptions about stress, 7

Normal response, stress as, 22

On Death and Dying, Kubler-Ross, 111
Opening Up, Pennebaker, 105
Optimism, 58

Pennebaker
    disclosure as tool, 71, 104, 108
    Opening Up, 105
    puritan health ethic, 54
    studies of effects on health, 71
Performance
    signs of stress, 30
    zone of peak, 21
Personality and stress, 39
Perspiration, increases as response to stress, 19, 29
Physical
    diseases linked to stress, 37
    relaxation, 88, 91
    Seesaw law, 24
    signs of stress, 29, 89
    stress reaction, 14, 16
Pierce, *Eat Your Stress Away*, 3
Positive beliefs, 86
Process, as, 11
Professional resources, 130
Psychotherapy, 104
Pupils, dilation in response to stress, 18
Puritan health ethic, 54

Quiet zones and routine, 126

Rahe and Holmes, research by, 36
Rats, studying stress in, 16, 36
Reactions, part of process, 12
Recovery from loss, 110
Reduction of stress
    appropriate responses, 23
    techniques, 53

Reflections on Healing and Regeneration, Cousins, 85
Relationship signs of stress, 30
Relaxation, 88, 91
    alternate with periods of stress, 23
    contract, 102
    guidelines, 94
    mind, of, 96
    response, 51
Resistance phase of stress response, 26
Responses to stress
    pattern of, 17
    phases, 25
    typical, 18
Routine, 126
    filofax technique, 122
    value of, 128
Rumination, 49
Ruthe, observations of, 60

Saltman, *With a Little Help*, 131
Seesaw law, 24
Self-criticism, 76
Self-talk, 72, 120
Seligman
    The Effectiveness of Psychotherapy, 105
    What You Can Change and What You Can't, 58
Selye
    research by, 36
    The Stress of Life, 10, 16
Sensory awareness training, 92
Services for help, 130
Shorter, *From Paralysis to Fatigue*, 55
Signs
    relaxation, 91
    stress, 28, 29, 89
Sleep, stress-free, 123
Sport, application of Yerkes-Dodson law, 21, 73
Startle reflex, 25
Stearns, *Coming Back*, 108
Strength, hysterical, 24
Stress and Distress, Brew, 48
Stress and Psychiatric Disorder, Tanner, 42
Stress-free sleep, 123
Stress mapping, 113
Stressors, 9, 11
    multiple, 24

Stress reduction techniques, 53
Stress response
    alarm phase, 25
    exhaustion phase, 27
    hyper-reactive, 25
    inhibited, 51
    resistance phase, 26
    suppression of, 27
    unconscious, 27
    war, during, 25
Strong feelings, dealing with, 104
Stupid stoppers, 75
    disputing, 83
Sudden death syndrome, 32
Suicide, impact of stress on, 38
Suppression, Obsession etc, Wegner, 97
Symptoms, 9, 11, 12

Tanner, *Stress and Psychiatric Disorder*, 42
TEN DAY DE-STRESS PLAN, Kenton, 3
Tension
    letting go, 90, 98
    physical signs of, 89
Thalamic response, ability to alter, 49
The Broken Heart, Lynch, 36
The Effectiveness of Psychotherapy,
    Seligman, 105
The Less Stress Book, guide to using, 3
The Social Readjustment Rating Scale, 37
The Relaxation Response, Benson, 51
The Stress of Life, Selye, 10, 16
Thinking
    changing, 49, 68
    high and low level, 47
    traps, recognising, 79
Thoughts
    becoming aware of, 81
    capturing, diary method, 79
    hurtful, 72
    mental rehearsal of, 86
    unconscious, 70

Time distortion at times of extreme
    stress, 20
To Have or To Be, Fromm, 63
Toads, recommendations regarding, 86
Traps, recognising, 79
Tupling, *A Weight off Your Mind*, 3
Type A personality
    dangerous drivers, 74
    filofax technique, 122
    heart disease and stress, 39,
Typical responses to stress, 18

Unconscious
    incompetence, 69
    stress response, 27
    thought, 70
Unmasking the Face, Ekman, 28

Views on stress, 6
Visual distortion at times of extreme
    stress, 20

War, potentation of stress response, 25
Wegner, *White Bear. Unwanted
    Thoughts*, 97
What You Can Change and What You Can't,
    Seligman, 58
White tornado, method of imaging, 101
With a Little Help, Saltman, 131
Working environment
    cultural messages in, 33
    quiet zones in, 127
    stress, 33, 115

Yerkes-Dodson law, 21, 72, 91
Your Body: Biofeedback at its Best,
    Jenks, 101

Zone
    peak performance, 21
    quiet, 126